"With the gift of his experien
Bowman's exquisite vulneral
understanding, better advoca
sion that moves beyond stere
director, a mother to an autistic child, and a Jesus follower, I have
been waiting for a book like *On the Spectrum*. This is the book the
church has desperately needed. I want to give this book to everyone I know."

MW00987157

—**Nish Weiseth**, founder and spiritual director,
Formation Northwest

"Bowman invites readers into another way of looking at the world,
literature, and faith through his artful and thoughtful eyes. It's
both a gift and an indictment of our world to experience how
autistic people navigate a society, including the church, that is not
set up for them to thrive. I hope everyone reads this book and the
many others that are sure to come."

—**D. L. Mayfield**, author of *The Myth of the American Dream:
Reflections on Affluence, Autonomy, Safety, and Power*

"In his remarkable meditations on autistic life, Bowman creates a
living map to orient newcomers to our neurodiverse world. I cannot
imagine a better guide than his generously empathic and richly detailed writing. *On the Spectrum* is essential reading, perhaps especially for well-meaning Christians whose limited conception of the
imago Dei has failed to recognize the divine hand in neurodiversity."

—**Amy Sullivan**, religion journalist; author of *The Party Faithful*

"A deft and poetic affirmation of faith, Bowman's new book is able
to 'honor autistic lives—breathed by the very breath of God—that
often feel fragile in the exacting landscape of an allistic world.'
Bowman accomplishes this through a pondering of self: a journey
through his life, his connection to story, and his search for tran-
scendence. Bowman creates a kenotic text: a book that shows us
how to respect 'one's personhood, to listen, to default to humility
and kindness.'"

—**Nick Ripatrazone**, author of *Wild Belief*;
culture editor for *Image Journal*

"June Jordan tells us that practicing poetry means taking control
of the language of your life. Bowman exemplifies what this task
looks and feels like while inviting us to bear witness, alongside
him, to the minute particulars of being human. By picking up what

he's setting down, we're enjoined in the work of dwelling more knowingly in our own existence. Receive his voice."

—**David Dark**, author of *Life's Too Short to Pretend You're Not Religious*

"Combining narrative, poetry, found material, letters, analysis, and interviews, this book compels its readers into a story of art, a story of faith, and a story of a life. *Read and believe and act and change*, Bowman invites, not because his is the only word but because reading and believing and acting and changing is the only way our world can be made safer."

—**Pádraig Ó Tuama**, author of *In the Shelter*

"In fresh, clear, and crisp prose, Bowman takes us on a journey— his life is a living map—a revelation of the deepest essence of his being as an autistic person. Not only did his narratives educate me further about neurodiversity, they compelled me to pause in awe and wonder, in contemplation, as I considered the spectrum of beauty and wisdom contained within these pages. Bowman deftly demonstrates that each of us has a place in this neurodiverse world. This book is a great gift."

—**Marlena Graves**, author of *The Way Up Is Down: Becoming Yourself by Forgetting Yourself*

"Moving from mere acceptance to unabashed celebration of neurodiversity is a long overdue and necessary shift; truly, I believe this is an invitation from the Holy Spirit. I am so grateful to Bowman for searingly and beautifully sharing his own fearfully-and-wonderfully-made story and inviting all of us to a more full, more diverse, more compelling vision of the kingdom of God."

—**Sarah Bessey**, editor of *A Rhythm of Prayer*; author of *Jesus Feminist*

"Using the metaphor of a plum tree growing in an inhospitable environment, and with a poet's eye for detail, Bowman engages different modes of interacting with the world and its multifarious senses. A sense of vigilance pervades the quiet universe of language unfolding in his soul, whether in church, outdoors in a field, or within a community of artists. Bowman reminds us of the role of poetry and faith in guiding us toward God and ultimately in honoring the dignity of our shared humanity."

—**Karen An-hwei Lee**, author of *The Maze of Transparencies* and *Phyla of Joy*

ON THE SPECTRUM

Previous Books by the Author

A Plum Tree in Leatherstocking Country

ON THE SPEC TRUM

Autism, Faith, and the Gifts of Neurodiversity

Daniel Bowman Jr.

BrazosPress

a division of Baker Publishing Group
Grand Rapids, Michigan

Published by Brazos Press
a division of Baker Publishing Group
PO Box 6287, Grand Rapids, MI 49516-6287
www.brazospress.com

Printed in the United States of America

Library of Congress Cataloging-in-Publication Data
Names: Bowman, Daniel, Jr., 1977– author.
Title: On the spectrum : autism, faith, and the gifts of neurodiversity / Daniel
    Bowman, Jr.
Description: Grand Rapids, Michigan : Brazos Press, a divion of Publishing Group,
    [2021] | Includes bibliographical references.
Identifiers: LCCN 2021019210 | ISBN 9781587435065 (paperback) | ISBN
    9781587435317 (casebound) | ISBN 9781493431120 (ebook)
Subjects: LCSH: Autism—Religious aspects—Christianity. | Autism spectrum
    disorders. | Neurobehavioral disorders—Patients—Rehabilitation.
Classification: LCC RC553.A88 D36 2021 | DDC 616.85/882—dc23
LC record available at https://lccn.loc.gov/2021019210

The author is represented by WordServe Literary Group (www.wordserveliterary.com).

21 22 23 24 25 26 27   7 6 5 4 3 2 1

CONTENTS

Prelude: You Always Hurt the Ones You
    Love   9

Foundations

Why You Should Read This Book (and
    How)   35

Diversity and Dignity   46

Speaking the Words   49

A Portrait of the Autist as a Young Man   55

The Neurodiversity Paradigm   63

Place

Living Maps   77

Autistic Culture Making   90

Riding while Autistic   101

Community, Worship, and Service

Autism and Church   109

Shining like the Sun   114

Contents

Service and the Spectrum   121

Dancing in Fields of Wheat and Tares   131

Writing, Teaching, and Learning

Autism and Poetry   139

The Insidious Nature of Bad Christian
    Stories   143

Beautiful Loser   149

Meaning and Estrangement   153

The Tracks of My Tears   160

Family and Identity

A True Name   165

Loving the Expanse   181

Peace in Terabithia   184

Spectrum Interviews

Interview by Molly   191

Interview by Jenna   203

Interview by Brian   209

New Directions

Falling and Autistic Representation   219

Therefore Let Us Keep the Feast   225

SEND and the Future of Neurodiversity   233

Acknowledgments   243

Notes   245

PRELUDE

You Always Hurt the Ones You Love: Crisis, Diagnosis, Hope

The temptation is to make an idol of our own experience, to assume our pain is more singular than it is. . . . Experience means nothing if it does not mean beyond itself: *we* mean nothing unless and until our hard-won meanings are internalized and catalyzed within the lives of others. There is something I am meant to see, something for which my own situation and suffering are the lens, but the cost of such seeing—I am just beginning to realize—may very well be any final clarity or perspective on my own life, my own faith. That would not be a bad fate, to burn up like the booster engine that falls away from the throttling rocket, lighting a little dark as I go.

—Christian Wiman, *My Bright Abyss*

As we shape our stories, we shape ourselves.

—Virginia Stem Owens,
"Narrating Our Lives"

October 2019

The last suitcase has been packed into the car. The odometer on our 2006 Honda shows nearly 300,000 miles, but we trust it as much as ever; it took us safely to Sarasota, Atlanta, Charleston, Baltimore, New York, and back home again just a few months ago. This trip, Beth and the kids are visiting our friends who moved to North Carolina after eight years here in Indiana, eight years of developing the most cherished relationship we've ever known as a family. I ache to see our friends too, but my fall break at the university does not come for a few more weeks, so I must stay home.

I'm sitting at our dining room table in my usual seat. The house looks different when I'm about to be alone. Details suddenly jump out at me: the original oak framework on the pocket doors, the 1950s rose-vine wallpaper, the 1930s Wurlitzer our daughter Una plays every day. I like telling guests—especially my English majors—that the house was built in 1890, the same summer that Oscar Wilde's masterpiece *The Picture of Dorian Gray* was published in *Lippincott's Monthly Magazine*.

The romance of this knowledge is lost in life's dailiness: running Una to play rehearsals and jazz band, or Casey to robotics club; Beth's baking bread or writing poems; my grading another freshman essay that begins with, "In society today . . ." But just now the house and its history feel important. They crystallize in the shadow of a coming loneliness.

I try to thwart the melancholy with an ambitious mental list of things I'll do this week. Certainly I'll catch up on schoolwork. I can probably finish the new Ta-Nehisi Coates book. I need to call my mom. And it wouldn't hurt to jog a few miles.

In reality, I'll clean the house obsessively to exert maximum control over my environment. I'll somehow fall further behind on schoolwork because . . . because I always do. I will put off all phone calls and texts as they'll feel unbearable. An indiscriminate number of episodes of shows Beth doesn't care for (spy thrillers, sci-fi) will form the backdrop of my evenings. I'll stay up too late staring into screens with near-absolute lack of purpose, counting down the hours until I'm no longer alone.

Every day of the week I will remind myself, over and over, that this leaving is okay. This one is good and right and temporary, and I don't need to be scared. Yet my body won't respond to reason; it has a memory of its own.

This is not like that other leaving, I tell myself, the memory of which makes the back of my neck go cold.

. . .

As if reading my mind, Beth puts her hand on my shoulder. She's cautious, but I also detect a playful warmth.

"Love you," she says.

It sends me. It always has.

It doesn't come a lot. At times it has stopped coming altogether. Sometimes in its place is its ugly opposite (accompanied once by a household object zipping past my ear).

The memories give me pause. I have deserved it if anyone has. I have caused pain; what's more, I've caused trauma. I never meant to, but as the Mills Brothers sang in 1944, "You Always Hurt the One You Love," and there's dark, knotty truth in that.

There's a particularly autistic way this hurting happens—inadvertently, mostly—by virtue of the fact that what autistics need so deeply, just to function from moment to moment, seems often to run counter to what people need from us. Maybe we need structure and predictability at the very time the people in our lives need whim, impulse. Maybe we need to be alone when they long for companionship. Maybe our senses are overloaded when theirs are underwhelmed. It can seem like we're acting unkindly, or worse; though almost always we're just trying to survive in a world that was not made for the likes of us.

Of course, before you have a diagnosis, you don't know any of this. You can't know. The story you tell yourself about yourself, the story that shapes you, is that you're not normal, that you're an awful human being: a lousy friend, a terrible husband, even a bad parent. You think you're letting everyone down, and that maybe the people in your life would be better off without you.

For those of us who follow Christ, we believe we're doing *that* badly too, that pursuit that informs all others—we're laying waste to a witness in the world.

We ask God, "Where are you?"

We live with intense guilt and shame. One study of autistic adults released by Anglia Ruskin University in Cambridge confirms: "Dr. Steven Stagg, Senior Lecturer in Psychology, said, 'One aspect of the research I found heart-wrenching was that the participants had grown up believing they were bad people. They referred to themselves as *alien* and *non-human*.'"[1]

The study also says that many of us are treated for depression. Other studies show that the suicide rate for autistic people is ten times higher than that of our allistic peers, and that the average life expectancy of the autistic person is just thirty-six years.[2]

. . .

As the hugs end, the car doors close and the engine starts. My wife and our children drive away. I am alone now, trying not to remember that other leaving, the one that would change everything, that would set me on a path toward answers I didn't know existed.

November 2014

I'm sitting on the edge of the bed in a dimly lit second-floor hotel room on Sanibel Island, Florida. I'm here for a writer's conference. I've come mostly to meet Richard Russo, Pulitzer Prize winner and hero to literary-minded central New Yorkers like me. Russo grew up just a few exits down the Thruway from mine. His first novel even bears the name of my hometown: *Mohawk*.

Mohawk is Beth's hometown too. Her parents still live there, in the same house on Church Street where she grew up. The house where she and our two kids are staying right now, have been staying since she left our home, left Indiana, left me.

. . .

We had a fight on our way to the Indianapolis airport. I experienced what I would later call an extreme autistic meltdown. But at the time, neither of us truly knew what had happened or why. Both of us were devastated. Because I was the one channeling the demons, I would need to accept the blame. I would need to be left.

You have heard it said that anger is fear's bodyguard. But I say to you that anger is fear's body *double*, its evil twin. They dress in each other's clothes; no one can distinguish between them, penetrate the veneer to understand the primal reactions below the surface. No one knows there is a veneer. At its best (or worst), the ruse is complete, the power absolute.

If I'm talking in abstractions here, it's for at least two reasons: (1) I still don't understand the outright terror that exists for me in meltdowns. I don't really know how to talk about them, and I'm a little scared to, as though I might somehow afford them even more influence. I know that's absurd, but my meltdowns have threatened to undo me. In them I have seen hell. (2) The nature of meltdowns is as close to an out-of-body experience as I've had. I honestly don't remember the details after. They seem to be a last-resort regulatory mechanism, a shocking reset button for the nerve endings. When I come to, I'm prickly, rumpled, dazed.

Autistic writer Ashlea McKay describes her meltdowns as "emotional avalanches," saying, "They can happen at any time and can be caused by a number of factors, including environmental stimuli, stress, uncertainty, rapid and impactful change, and much more." She talks about her heart pounding, throat drying up, tears falling, senses blasting, the room spinning.[3] Kaleb Johnson, describing what happens after the onslaught of unwanted input, simply says, "[Sometimes] I pass out. My brain gives up trying to fight."[4]

Suffice it to say that these are punishing events, and we don't have control over them. But again: how could anyone expect to know what's unfolding when you don't know you're autistic? Back to thinking you're a horrible person, some sort of insane loose cannon.

Back to depression. Back to suicidal ideation.

Which brings us back to the dimly lit hotel room on Sanibel Island.

. . .

It is the worst day of my life. I am positive that I cannot live without Beth and our two beautiful children. The only thing on my mind is quitting this life. I plan to get up from the bed, walk across the patio (past the perky orange lounge chairs with drink holders) to the water's edge, and enter the Gulf of Mexico until the saltwater fills my lungs, claims me, ends me.

I don't want to write this down, now or ever. This is not a story I want to tell myself or anyone else. I want to protect my kids from it, whatever that means. But I need to tell the truth. So if someday my kids do read this account, I will trust them to feel their feelings, to come to terms with these realities, to mourn my past—their past—as I have. It is awful and there's no way around it but through it.

I want to walk into the water, but my body is frozen to the bed. I sit motionless for well over an hour.

I move only to turn off the light and lie down. When I sleep, I do not dream.

. . .

Earlier in the day I'd decided to go to the opening session of the conference. After all, it's why I came. A well-known writer spoke about . . . some element of storytelling, I suppose. I didn't hear a word because I sat apart from everyone and listened through earbuds on full volume to a recording of a honey-voiced therapist talking through deep-breathing exercises. The recording had come preloaded on a tiny black MP3 player a counselor on my campus had given me some months before as he ushered me kindly out the door. I'd been more depressed than usual, and so he'd agreed to let me stop in and see if he could make a referral. His job included triage for anyone—faculty, staff, and students—but long-term treatment was for students only.

I'd jammed the MP3 player into the bottom of my backpack and thought nothing of it until my plane landed in Florida and somehow it popped into my mind. I checked to see if it was still there. Of course it was; I never clean out my backpack.

I don't know if the breathing exercises worked, but I did them religiously because I couldn't think of anything else to do to not die. In that sense, I guess they did work.

Why wouldn't my body move toward the sea that night? I'd rehearsed the act in my mind, and nothing would have stopped me from carrying it out. I knew not a soul on the entire island; I was a perfect stranger to everyone at the conference and the hotel. It was dark out and the beach was empty. It would have been easy.

My body wouldn't cooperate. Something stopped it from happening. Was it merely the inexorable pull of Doing Stuff? Setting an alarm, getting up in the morning, dutifully attending sessions at the conference, eating, brushing my teeth? Was it just my autistic need for structure, routine, control? Did I make a choice—conscious or otherwise—to live? Did God save me? I don't know.

I lived. In a few days I came home. And a few weeks later, Beth and the kids came home. Though there would be much work ahead of us, it was the best day of my life.

January 2015: Self-Diagnosis

I had my life back, but I still had no explanation for who I was, or *how* I was who I was.

I needed a new story that could shape my future and—though I didn't know to want such a thing—perhaps reframe my past.

All I knew was that the old story, the only one I had, was not right. It didn't hold up. It just said that much of what I felt and did was wrong and bad, and that when I broke down, it got ugly. That's not much of a story to go on. What if instead I had something with a name, something clinical—something treatable? I needed the promise of better days ahead. I needed a new lifeline to the master narrative I had long believed in: the story of a fall, yes, but also redemption and purpose. I needed a second chance.

I launched into an intense monthslong search. Greater self-awareness became my obsession. I would figure this out so I wouldn't be doomed to repeat my mistakes and keep hurting the ones I love.

. . .

I was not put off by the idea of counseling; after all, I'd been a longtime adherent to the practice of spiritual direction. Back in New York, I met monthly for nearly five years with a pastor-writer, a doctor of ministry from Princeton Theological Seminary. He codirected a nonprofit called Life Listening, and his philosophy of spiritual direction was based on their tag-line: "Helping you listen to your life." Our times together were shaped by a process of increasing intentionality, recognizing the patterns I fell into (for better or worse), and making decisions toward healthier daily practices, including serving others.

My spiritual director was well-versed in tools like the Enneagram, adopting it as a discernment method years before it caught on in evangelical circles. He and his wife also had a labyrinth in their backyard. I walked it and prayed. But mostly we talked. Well, I talked and he listened, and I listened to myself, to the rhythms of my days and nights, to the pulses of my relationships, to the cadences of the divine. For as Paula D'Arcy has said, "God comes to us disguised as our life."[5]

Looking back, it seems incredible to me that neither my spiritual director nor I recognized symptoms of what was then called Asperger syndrome. Yet that lack of awareness is indicative of the sheer absence of understanding of the autism spectrum (especially as it affects adults) even into the early 2000s, an absence that is only now beginning to abate. At the time, we had no familiarity with the terminology, how autism presented, or why it might explain so much of my identity. If you'd asked me about it, I would have pictured a child, one with "special needs" who was probably getting into trouble in school or sitting alone, rocking back and forth on the floor. Or—I have to say it—Dustin Hoffman in *Rain Man*. I wasn't a child with special needs and I wasn't a math genius, so autism never crossed my mind.

Later, when I moved to Indiana to begin my professorship, I discovered that the John XXIII Center, a retreat house down the street, also offered spiritual direction. I set up an appointment. My spiritual director during those years was a member of an order called the Poor Handmaids of Jesus Christ, a group originating in Dernbach, Germany, in the mid-nineteenth century. (Their foundress was, in fact, canonized as Saint Katharina Kasper in October 2018 by Pope Francis.)

The sisters landed in the American Midwest upon being called to aid the settlement of German immigrants in Hessen Cassel, Indiana, in 1868. I felt very fortunate in relocating to a rural heartland town that had somehow intersected with a fascinating group of devout Christ followers, women who offered a substantive history and current record of service, counsel, retreat work, and more. Sister Joetta and I lit candles and prayed together; we talked and listened and reasoned and consulted Scripture. Sometimes I cried. I grew in new ways during this time. But again, the hours I spent with her would also prove unable to breach the walls of an enormous underlying reality of my life: my autistic brain wiring.

. . .

In January 2015, as if making a high-stakes New Year's resolution to discover my own identity, I wrestled hard with the torments that had long plagued me. I read a great deal and pressed further than ever before into my anger, fear, depression, and anxiety. Those struggles played some part in my journey, to be sure—only I didn't realize they were mere effects of a deeper cause.

That strange word—*autism*—would only come into my life after weeks of prayer and study. I stumbled across the idea down some online rabbit hole—so deep, in fact, that I don't remember how I landed there. But from the moment I began reading about it, I realized it fit. Perfectly. So perfectly I was dumbfounded. Of course I never knew I was supposed to be looking, but still. Now it seemed glaringly obvious. And because it was true, because it was an important truth, God was in it. This was the beginning of an enormous change in how I thought about myself.

In his book *The Journal of Best Practices: A Memoir of Marriage, Asperger Syndrome, and One Man's Quest to Be a Better Husband*, David Finch describes the time when his wife, who happened to be an autism expert, decided to confirm her suspicions about him. She sat him down to ask a series of questions that might begin a journey toward a better place.

I connected with his astonishment at the profound acumen into his life the questions offered:

"Do you tend to get so absorbed by your special interests that you forget or ignore everything else?" . . .

"Special interests?"

"You know," she said, "things like practicing your saxophone for four hours a day, or when you wrote scenes at the Second City and I hardly ever saw you . . ."

"Oh, well, sure," I said. "I mean, doesn't everybody get into stuff?"

"No," she replied. . . . "Many people can do something they enjoy and not let it consume their whole life so they forget to pay bills, or put on shoes, or check in on their family from time to time."

Later in the same scene, he becomes ever more dazzled by how on-the-nose the questions are:

"Before doing something or going somewhere, do you need to have a picture in your mind of what's going to happen so as to prepare yourself mentally first?"

This question seems rather insightful. "O-oh my God," I stammered. "Yeah, that's totally me."

"Do you prefer to wear the same clothes and eat the same food every day? Do you become intensely frustrated if an activity that is important to you gets interrupted? Do you have strong attachments to certain favorite objects?"

"Those are all yes."

"I know. Do you have certain routines which you need to follow? Do you get frustrated if you can't sit in your favorite seat?"

"I have literally ended friendships over the seat thing. . . ."

"Do you feel tortured by clothes tags, clothes that are too tight or are made from the 'wrong' material? Do you tend to shut down or have a meltdown when stressed or overwhelmed?"

All yes. But I was too stunned to answer aloud.[6]

I shared his amazement as I read his book and others. I spent weeks reading everything I could get my hands on about autism, from clinical books like Tony Attwood's *The Complete Guide to Asperger's Syndrome* to newer own-voices narratives like Temple Grandin's *Thinking in Pictures* and Cynthia Kim's *Nerdy, Shy, and Socially Inappropriate: A User Guide to an Asperger Life*. I gleaned understanding from each and grew toward greater self-knowledge.

Self-assurance, on the other hand, did not come as quickly. Though I knew for certain by this time that I was autistic, I was afraid to begin opening up about it. How, precisely, had my story changed? How would I tell people? What would they think? It would take time to unpack.

I reread the autism section of the Diagnostic and Statistical Manual of Mental Disorders (DSM–5) very carefully. Prior to 2013, I would've been diagnosed with Asperger's, but the hundreds of clinicians and mental health professionals who contributed to the DSM–5 had made a somewhat radical and, in some circles, controversial decision to fold Asperger's into the broader "autism spectrum." After looking over the criteria for an autism diagnosis dozens of times, I knew without a doubt that I had a place on that spectrum, and I was just beginning to grasp its contours.

. . .

Around this time, I stumbled across a book that illuminated those contours in a new way, a book that spoke to me intimately and helped assuage my fears that autism was something only for techies in Silicon Valley or oddball math savants. *Writers on the Spectrum: How Autism and Asperger Syndrome Have Influenced Literary Writing* by Julie Brown gave me so much hope. While many books used examples of autistics drawn to science and technology (Finch himself studied music engineering technology and describes himself as a "math nerd"), Brown's book focused on novelists, poets, and essayists whom the scholar strongly suspected of being autistic, and she provided compelling evidence.

Nothing nourished me more. Within a few short months of understanding autism as the underlying operating system that ran my brain, I was also thrilled to put myself in the probable company of Emily Dickinson, Herman Melville, William Butler Yeats, and others. I was like them, in neurotype if not talent. They were weird, to be sure, but *literary* weird, my favorite kind.

Brown cites professor Michael Fitzgerald, who "argued that certain features of [autism], such as persistence, singlemindedness, intelligence, and nonconformity, can enhance not just the analytical process, but the creative process as well."[7] While the practice of retrodiagnosis certainly has its drawbacks, it's tough to argue with the logic here, and it was a line of thinking that offered me important affirmation as an autistic artist.

Each of these books and others—plus a weekly diet of dozens of online articles and essays—kept me learning, growing, obsessing, and confirming. At this point, there was not a sliver of lingering doubt in my mind that I was autistic. I journaled about the feeling of having been in the dark for so long:

> I can see the big picture of autism now. Life before was—to cite an image I read recently—like a series of car accidents: each day when I woke up and entered the world, I crashed again, often badly. Only I couldn't tell from one day to the next that I was prone to these accidents. I didn't remember yesterday's crash, or the day before's—I knew only a vague malaise, an undercurrent

of misery like a Tuesday in late January: dark, cold, inconvenient, unknowable. I had a sense that other crashes had been, but I perceived no pattern. I was the antithesis of a forensic crime-scene analyst on a ten o'clock police procedural: while they worked to collect and connect the dots, even the smallest, I walked by in a fog, not knowing there were any dots at all.

Despite my deepened comprehension, I started feeling that I could open up to family and friends better if I had a professional opinion—a medical diagnosis—not just my own ideas to proffer. And if I'm honest, I wanted something I could point to that might exonerate me of my past behavior, that might indicate a cause that superseded my own choices. I began the process of lining up new, often pricey, visits to my general practitioner and what would become a string of other professionals.

Spring 2015: Affirmation

The first counselor I connected with had an office at a large family practice in nearby Muncie, Indiana. She was nice but unhelpful and underprepared to deal with the spectrum (she said so on my first visit). But I thought the sessions might be worthwhile anyway, so I continued.

After I'd been seeing her for several months, she told me without warning that she was quitting the profession to take a better-paying job in the business world. She brought me immediately into the office of another counselor, who shook my hand and asked about making an appointment. The change was so abrupt and jarring, I couldn't speak. I smiled weakly, nodded my head to his idea to stop at the front desk and schedule a visit, then walked out the doors and never returned.

At the time I didn't know how to advocate for myself, to think through what might best meet my needs and pursue it. I felt lost in the world of mental health care.

A few weeks later I screwed my courage to the sticking place and made an appointment, via the despised telephone, with another counselor. When the day arrived, I got lost on my way there, then had trouble finding parking, so I ran in the door late, sweating, hoping someone would welcome me, tell me it's fine, and point me to the water cooler—invite me to sit and relax a minute. Instead the nurse at the front desk, by way of a greeting, insisted on a pop-up drug test as soon as I checked in. To call it unnerving would be an understatement. I felt like a criminal, having the burden of proof placed on my shoulders—or more precisely, in a plastic cup.

Exiting the restroom, I handed the urine sample to the now-gloved nurse, who was standing attentively by the door. I was escorted down several hallways to my new counselor's office for the inaugural session. She began talking immediately, devoid of introduction or warmth. The therapist, a beautiful woman with bright blue eyes who looked not much older than me, launched into a disconcerting rapid-fire question-answer game. Only, unlike the helpful questions David Finch's wife asked, I rarely saw the point of any of these. She looked at me with a detached air, not a polite objectivity but an arrogant remoteness, like I was a zoo animal or an amoeba under her microscope.

She continued to shoot all sorts of questions at me, talking quickly, periodically looking down at a script, and not seeming to listen much to my answers. An impenetrable coldness pervaded the room. It put me on a tense edge (I guess that was the point?). And then, when I thought things couldn't get worse, she began mixing in math problems. I wondered what kind of bastard clinician had invented this form of torture; it was not something I'd encountered in any of my reading. I played it out as long as I could, hopeful that some slipup I made would indicate something useful to her (and finally, to me).

"Tell me more about your relationship with your brother," she asked.

"Well, we're two years apart in age, so we played together a lot when we were—"

"—What's twelve times nine?" she interjected, glaring into my eyeballs.

"Um. Huh?" I hesitated. I'd started feeling like I'd been lotteried into some kind of Mental Health Hunger Games, and now my life was on the line for reasons I couldn't understand.

I left in a hurry and did not go back, ever. Surely someone out there had to be better than this. Or was I a freak to be studied from a distance—is that what I signed up for? I chose hope. I thought, there must be someone who is qualified and knowledgeable and also *kind*, who will treat me as an equal, or at least as a person.

I finally visited a psychiatrist, who was skeptical of my self-diagnosis and refused to listen to my reasoning. He put me on and off a number of different meds and dosages for generalized anxiety, then depression, and finally diagnosed me as bipolar. This diagnosis was his great contribution to my care, and I appreciate it to this day.

However, my psychiatrist refused to do any counseling, and the counselors I'd seen were not licensed to prescribe meds. So under this system, one professional has the power to alter your brain chemistry without much understanding of who you are, while another might learn about you but is powerless to do much except listen. Which is not nothing, but also doesn't represent the highest level of treatment one needs.

I tried one more local counselor, whom I chose because he was close to my workplace and free, and I couldn't justify spending more money without exhausting all my available resources. The center was staffed by MA students at a nearby college who were gaining experience as part of their credentialing process. I knew right away it wouldn't work. My counselor, a thoughtful if somewhat dubious twentysomething sporting a ponytail and acne, looked too much like my own students. Far worse was that he knew next to nothing helpful about autistic adults. I'd gleaned more in my reading than everything he knew put together; he admitted this within the first ten minutes.

I made it through several sessions simply on the strength of hearing myself talk out loud about my life through the new lens of autism. The words and phrases I used were often borrowed from things I'd read, but that's not to say they didn't carry an air of authority. They sometimes sounded strange and exotic to my ears, but also intimate and true. I was shaping this new story, and in turn, my new life.

But after three appointments, I had no plans to return to this particular counselor either, and once again I was further demoralized by the stark realities of the disjointed, dysfunctional mental health world. Could anyone help me? Was there any method in this madness?

. . .

So as if in search for the Holy Grail, I went big. I tracked down a therapist who was the most qualified autism expert I could find, a PhD whose office was in one of the most expensive suburbs of Indianapolis. She didn't take my insurance, so I paid her a hundred and fifty dollars per session, in cash, and when I ran out of money, I charged it on my credit card. I told her everything about me and attended enough sessions until she could tell me if, in her (highly credible) professional opinion, I was on the autism spectrum. In the end I got what I'd come for: she said she had no doubt I was autistic. I walked out and, as was now my habit, never went back.

As for me: I knew the next step. I would need to make peace with the diagnosis. That meant I would need to write about it, to describe my way of being in the world (my "symptoms") on the page. I would need to claim that word *autism* as fully as I could now. The following is the first blog post I finished—my new story as best as I knew it.

Fall 2015

I am autistic.

I am ready to write about it.

I'm ready, I think, but the topic overwhelms me; it will take multiple essays to start a proper exploration. In her 2014 memoir, Cynthia Kim wrote that since her diagnosis, "In a way, I've been forced to relearn how to be me."[8] That feels right. The facts of being me have not changed, but the meanings of those facts have undergone a great shift, "a sea-change, into something rich and strange," to quote famous lines from *The Tempest*.

I still don't know what to make of this shift, even after diagnosis, even after reading many books and articles about the autism spectrum, talking with therapists and a small inner circle, and considering this all in journaled words that will remain private.

I don't know where to begin, but I know what I feel and have always felt: alienation, an estrangement so powerful that I barely feel like a person sometimes. So I guess I'll start there.

. . .

It's rare that I can forget how different I am from the people around me and how much that has hurt at every stage of my life. And meaningful relationships—those time-honored antidotes to alienation—can be, in a cruel irony, difficult for people on the spectrum to achieve and maintain, per the very nature of our impairments.

How am I alienated? Let me count the ways.

Social settings, from the simplest hello to a small dinner to complex, manifold gatherings full of strangers, can induce lopsided levels of anxiety. I've learned to fake—mask—an appearance of normalcy, but I may well be crawling out of my skin—not because I don't want to be there but because I don't know *how*.

My senses are unusually deft, and combinations of sounds, smells, and sights can put me into sensory overload quickly. If

I'm too warm, I won't be able to focus on anything until I can escape and cool down. I may get confused or say something awkward. I make little eye contact; if I am able to force it, I might drop it at a jarring moment. If you see me someplace and call out my name—or, God forbid, touch me—I will be startled to an unusual degree and not process who you are for at least a few seconds, leaving us both embarrassed.

If we enter into conversation, I may fidget and writhe, my head and back and shoulders saying I'm not interested, I'm angry, or nature is issuing a strong call. I'll try to hide my impatience with small talk and polite banter; my impulse is to cut to the things I obsess over, without transition: What are you reading? What are you writing? What moves you? Say things that are true and beautiful now. Be what I need you to be, not what you are. Listen as I prattle about obscure big band era musicians or the history of baseball. Oh and if you hurt my feelings I may retreat into absolute silence for long stretches, or just up and ghost you.

If I haven't pushed you away yet, I might if you see me blow on my knuckles, one hand at a time, left then right, then tap my legs with slightly closed fists. This one I will try, try so hard, to suppress. But it could happen. Or I'll stim in other, less obvious ways: I'll stand alone in the kitchen and eat half a jar of briny, salty pickles or even brinier, saltier olives stuffed with slick red pimentos. I'll cherish each small sting on the tongue.

. . .

I don't call my family or best friends. I don't answer the phone, ever.

I can't "just relax" or "stop being so sensitive," as I've been told to do my whole life. I'm generally unsure how to engage with anyone; I use intellect and imitation in place of the missing intuition, leaving me mentally and emotionally exhausted a lot of the time. I can carry an acute envy, and sometimes hatred, and sometimes admiration, for those who navigate the social spheres fluidly, easily, *naturally*—anyone who becomes energized by it, not depleted and demoralized.

For me, unplanned social interactions, especially with new people, are like putting together a puzzle where the pieces are many and tiny; where you get the feeling early on that any number are missing; where the sky in the corner—all the pieces form white clouds and look exactly the same—has somehow grown larger in the time it took you to fit together a very obvious section of the border for which you feel disproportionately proud.

I have no spatial sense. I hate puzzles.

So I often give up, or never begin.

. . .

I'm a writer. I'm drawn to images that resonate at multiple levels. I've discovered that other autistic writers are too. In particular we gravitate toward metaphors, symbols, and narratives that represent or explore our profound differences from others. These symbols bring some order and meaning to the loneliness of being on the outside, misunderstood, rejected.

One of the symbols I developed in my first book of poems—long before I was diagnosed—is a small and odd fruit tree trying to survive in a cold climate. When I was a kid, a single plum tree graced the edge of my grandparents' field on Vickerman Hill Road, high above the Mohawk River Valley in upstate New York. Though not unheard of, any fruit tree other than apple is certainly delicate for the region, an eccentricity in the world of harsh Leatherstocking Country winters (California dominates plum growing in the US).

My grandparents' plum tree died. I loved that tree as one loves and admires the unusual, the improbable; I missed it when it was gone.

To reveal the symbol, let me talk briefly of men in the Mohawk Valley. My dad worked at the Union Tool Company, in

a forge making pitchforks and snow shovels and other implements with clear and practical purposes. His hands were not
merely calloused but often burned. Most of my friends' dads
worked at the Remington Arms Company, the longtime largest
employer in the valley. My uncles took apart and rebuilt cars,
trucks, motorcycles, lawnmowers, furnaces, hot water heaters.
This was the milieu of male identity in my home place.

Though I played a few sports and had some friends and
went to parties, I knew from a young age that I was not like
everyone else, that I would never grow up to be like the men I'd
known.

There was something different about me, something I could
never quite put my finger on. Like the plum tree, I was out of
place. I would chalk it up to my delicate artistic temperament;
I did, after all, become a poet. But with the revelation that I'm
autistic, the symbol of the plum tree took on another layer of
meaning.

Though it began as a personal image, I hope it can have some
universal import. The next generation back home—some of
whom by temperament, interests, sexual orientation, or physical or mental or neurobiological matters—may find themselves
alone in the valley like a plum tree in a field. They will not catch
footballs on the gridiron to their fathers' delight; they will not
squeeze into booths at the pizzeria; they will not make out in
Chevys by bonfires on the back roads. Maybe the plum tree
could stand for them too.

I continue to read clinical books on autism and memoirs of
lives lived on the spectrum. As a poet and novelist, one of the
most important books I've found is *Writers on the Spectrum*
by Julie Brown. Brown studies authors who, if they were alive
today, would be candidates for autism spectrum consideration,
as the records indicate clear correlations between autism and
the details of their lives and work. Their stories and lives—
like mine—are filled with awkward social moments, eccentric

and obsessive behavior, retreating from sensory overload, and, sometimes, an entire lifetime of loneliness.

Brown discusses the constant found in the writing:

> [The characters in these authors' stories] know that something about them is different. They feel that there is something wrong with them. They may or may not try to fit in, but if they do try to make a friend, they find that it isn't easy. There's no ignoring the messages of loneliness, sadness, or despair. . . . One thinks of Hans Christian Andersen's cold, wet, frozen characters struggling against the elements with no one to help them. One thinks of Bartleby, dying of a broken heart, all alone, in prison. Or Alice [in Wonderland], swimming in a lake of her own tears. One thinks of Sherwood Anderson's sad, oddball characters sitting by themselves in dilapidated shacks and upstairs apartments. The underlying message, again and again, is this: I am different and the world has rejected me.[9]

This passage gives me a feeling of warmth and camaraderie, assuaging my alienation in a peculiarly autistic way: though we're clinging to narratives with themes and symbols of isolation and despair, we're doing it together—if not *actually* together. We take refuge in images that become supremely important to our thinking, be it Emily Dickinson's small boat lost on a vast sea or William Butler Yeats's famous lake island.

For me it's a plum tree.

Still, while I find consolation in the symbol, I don't want to see it in merely one dimension. I want to work toward greater hope. Perhaps I can come to see the very planting of the plum tree as the optimistic gesture it surely was—an earnest, intentional attempt to cultivate something fragile, almost decadent, to counterbalance an exacting landscape.

Those of us on the spectrum will always deal with loneliness and alienation. Over time, though, maybe we can nurture the space to survive, even thrive, wherever we're planted.

November 2019

Una crashes the Wurlitzer, works her way through some *Newsies* and *Dear Evan Hansen* to limber her fingers for jazz band practice. The Christmas concert is just weeks away, and she's anchoring their set on keys, not to mention blocking the choreography for the show choir's opening number.

The winter sun bends through the dining room window at low angles, illuminates dusty framed pictures of Beth and me in college, posing ironically in ripped jeans and flannels. I never look into the camera.

Hearing his sister play, seeing me typing, and smelling fresh sourdough bread baking in the kitchen, Casey has given up hope of finding a partner for the next round of the everlasting game of Dutch Blitz. He pops in his earbuds, queues his Spotify playlist of electronica and video game music, and sprawls on his bedroom floor to build with LEGO bricks.

I reach back to four years ago, to the words of that first blog post about alienation. I feel the yearning and loss and uncertainty and naïve belief all over again. That post, written for *Ruminate* magazine, was my first attempt to say it on the page, to get to the heart of the matter. It led to many discussions with friends and some with strangers, in which I continued to hone my vision for myself, for my autistic life, for my roles as a husband, dad, writer, professor, and Christ follower. And it led to more posts and essays, some of which will appear in the following pages.

Some things have changed. Yet I continue wanting what I wanted then: to work toward greater hope; to thrive where I live and help others do the same; to honor autistic lives—breathed by the very breath of God—that often feel fragile in the exacting landscape of an allistic world.

FOUNDATIONS

The potential is great for the neurodiversity movement to create significant social transformation. . . . Neurodiversity brings with it a sense of hope that all individuals, regardless of how they read, think, feel, socialize, or attend, will be recognized for their gifts, and accorded the same rights and privileges as any other human being.

—Thomas Armstrong, "Neurodiversity:
A Concept Whose Time Has Come"

WHY YOU SHOULD READ THIS BOOK (AND HOW)

A Note to Neurotypical Readers

Thank you for meeting me here, for wanting to learn more about neurodiversity and people on the spectrum.

When you read an autistic memoir, you're not just getting an account of one life or gaining specialized knowledge about a tiny subsection of the population. You're learning about what it means to be human. You're learning about 1 in 45 people: friends, family, coworkers, children in school with your kids (or, like me, your kids' instructors), someone at church, and folks you encounter along the way—engineers and scientists, artists and writers, people who have helped shape our world.[1] You're learning how to love your neighbor as yourself. That's really the core of this book.

The Importance of #OwnVoices

In general, there are two kinds of nonfiction about autism: clinical books by researchers and doctors, and memoirs. The clinical books usually center on supporting autistic children, with autistic adults either entirely in the shadows or mentioned in passing. The memoirs are mostly written by parents of autistic kids, and only rarely written by autistic people. Memoirs tend to focus on helping neurotypical readers understand the autistic experience, or even just the experience of the caretakers of autistic children.

On the Spectrum is not quite either of those. It is, I hope, a book for a new era in thinking about autism, one increasingly defined by attention to diverse autistic voices ("Nothing about us without us," as the rallying cry goes)—#OwnVoices—and a greater comprehension and acceptance of the neurodiversity paradigm. The social media hashtag #OwnVoices was created by Corinne Duyvis, a Dutch autistic novelist of young adult books, to distinguish between books authored by someone in the same minority or disability category as the protagonist. This was a necessary step for autistic writers, as most books celebrated for their portrayals of autistic characters—for example, runaway bestseller *The Curious Incident of the Dog in the Night-Time* or the 2010 winner of the National Book Award for Young People's Literature, *Mockingbird*—are written by non-autistic authors.

Let's take a step back for a moment and consider that point: can you imagine another people group for whom that situation would be acceptable? Think, for example, if nearly all of the foremost texts of the Black American experience—the novels, memoirs, poems, and movies we teach our children—were written by white authors. It has been, thank God, a long time since we were in that situation. It would be unthinkable now. Or what if our most celebrated women characters in all of fiction were written by men? Also, thank God, unthinkable. No one would stand for that in the twenty-first century. Yet when it comes to autism, we're still giving out major awards to people who have never lived our experience but attempt to represent, perhaps even exploit, us.

Now you understand, I hope, why this book is needed. I'm tired of being spoken over by people with neurotypical brain wiring. You want to know what it's like in here? They can't tell you. I and my fellow autistic writers can speak for ourselves.

Full Immersion

Most of the essays in this collection touch directly on autism, while others enact my autistic experience more subtly through reflections on family and identity; the relationship between art and Christian faith; teaching, learning, and living in community; books and storytelling; and ordinary life in Middle America. This, too—this scope of the everyday—is critical.

Telltale signs of my autistic brain reveal themselves in many ways. Have you ever moved to a different region of the country? Did you read twenty-plus books about that new place because the move represented a dramatic upheaval of nearly impossible magnitude? Probably not. But that response is not unusual for an autistic person dealing with change. The essay "Living Maps" highlights the importance of such obsession in service of structure and routine for autistics.

Moving from the Northeast to the Midwest required my learning a whole new social system of manners and expectations; weather patterns; terrain and topography; a new job at a new university teaching new courses to a kind of learner who was also new to me; and of course new colleagues, friends, and acquaintances. The support available in reading the literature of place became a necessity—much more intricate than an intellectual exercise or gesture of goodwill toward the region.

So: please suppress the urge to skip ahead to the "more autistic" parts of this book. Every essay in the book is thoroughly autistic! More importantly: there are no shortcuts to learning how to love your neighbor. There is no list of action items, and there is no saying, "Just tell me what to do." What you can do is inhabit the whole story—and see the autistic heart, mind, body, and spirit at work in both the profound and the mundane.

Let me invite your attention another way.

As codirector of a national literary conference, I've booked many writers of color to speak at my campus. Most of them said to me, "Please don't bring me in just for another diversity panel." They followed up by telling me something they love and are good at but are never asked to speak about: French cuisine; poetry about pets; the history of vampire movies.

Asking them to speak only about race is telling them that I want to use them. In fact it's saying I have a very limited use for them. This is the opposite of honoring their full humanity, the imago Dei, including the work, and play, they've chosen for themselves.

Tokenization is a form of racism. Reducing an autistic person to bullet points is a form of ableism.

This is a memoir, a story of a life, and life rarely conforms to simple takeaways, no matter how badly we might want them when facing complexities beyond our grasp. Attention is the form of love called for here. Or let me borrow a strong symbol from my Baptist years: full immersion is what I'm asking for. Come down to the river to pray.

Autism and Neurodiversity

The phrase "the gifts of neurodiversity" appears in the subtitle. Neurodiversity's gifts do not form a discrete list. I think they are ways of being, of approaching our days; they are lenses through which the autistic person sees and feels the world uniquely—lenses that can lead to helpful contributions to culture. In my case, my autistic brain wiring leads me to see storytelling and poetry and teaching and learning and worshiping God in ways that are different from what most readers will be accustomed to. I hope you're open to exploring those ways alongside me, wherever they lead.

Neurodiversity may in fact be a new idea for some readers. It's not a scary or difficult concept; it simply means that there are different kinds of brains, different operating systems (OS) that run different people, to use a common, if simplistic, image. There's a *neurotypical* OS, which means that the brains of people in that group are similar, within a certain range. They are highly diverse in many aspects, and so they will function differently and yield different results, making for unique individuals. However, neurotypical brains are similar enough overall that the outcomes—neurotypical peoples' behaviors and actions and language—will mostly be considered "normal."

Then there's a *neurodivergent* operating system. It will result in people on the spectrum functioning in the intellectual, emotional, social, and physical realms differently from neurotypical people. Our actions and behaviors, then, should not be seen in light of the absence of neurotypical traits but instead the presence of autistic brain wiring.

When I talk about the pathology model or paradigm of viewing autism, I mean seeing an autistic OS and viewing it, and the results it produces, as *deficient* because it's not a neurotypical OS with neurotypical results. A laptop that runs Windows is not deficient just because it's not Mac OS, or vice versa; it's just a different operating system that functions in different ways. Overall, many of the needs of the average user—word processing, photo editing, web surfing, online collaboration—can be achieved by either OS, and even by other, more obscure operating systems.

So it is with neurodivergent persons: we have most of the same core features and bugs as anyone else. Our autism itself is our OS, not a bug.

Autistic brain wiring occurs naturally, not through insidious means like vaccines gone wrong or bad parenting. And it occurs in about 1 in every 45 people, regardless of race, ethnicity, culture, gender, and other factors. It's not true that there is "more autism than ever before"—there's *not* more than ever. It's that medical and psychology communities have grown better able to recognize and correctly diagnose it. Autism is simply more visible as a direct result of that knowledge.[2]

A neurodiversity paradigm asserts the basic fact that autism doesn't need to be fixed; it simply needs to be understood and accepted. This is important, because people who see it as needing to be fixed often put their autistic kids in tenuous situations like applied behavior analysis (ABA) "therapy." They often believe that their child needs, and will get, a new operating system—that the therapist will, if all goes well, replace the autistic brain wires with a neurotypical OS.

This kind of thinking is frankly foolish and deeply harmful. Many parents are scared when their kids begin in infancy or childhood to show common traits of autism; for example, self-regulatory behaviors, or *stimming*. Maybe they repeat a comforting phrase in an unusual tone while flapping their hands. Or maybe it's worse—maybe there are meltdowns that threaten harm to the child or others. The parents freak out and send their kids to ABA, assured by the practitioners that the therapy will stop those behaviors and make their child act "normal." A stated goal of ABA is to make autistic children "indistinguishable from their peers."

As the saying goes, be careful what you wish for.

ABA doesn't change an autistic into a neurotypical—it just teaches them to act neurotypical so they won't be punished. There are much healthier ways of accommodating an autistic person's differences and supporting them toward integration into society than the rewards-and-punishment system that is ABA. It's like conversion therapy for LGBTQ teens. It does not change their orientation and in fact inflicts lifelong trauma on most people who are subjected to it. Conversion therapy has been largely discredited by the medical community.

We are still mid-journey on the ABA front: many doctors and mental health experts do not know any other course of action, and ABA has yet to be supplanted by something healthier and widely recognized. Many doctors still recommend it to families searching for help. Universities training teachers and special education professionals still teach it.

One reason I wrote this book is to take part in leading from the inside. This is a case where you want to weigh medical advice with the hundreds of terrible stories told by autistic people themselves. I personally know many autistic adults who carry awful wounds from ABA, from therapists who punished them for stimming and other (normally) harmless behaviors that in fact—under the autistic OS—have purpose, meaning, and even richness. ABA causes trauma. Autistics don't need any more trauma than what we already attain from daily navigating a social world built by and for people with neurotypical brain wiring.

Form: On the Look and Feel of Autistic Narratives

Although I've revised this book for coherence, the essays touch on many different memories and topics, and they sometimes deviate from a larger narrative arc. As such, they reflect my autistic brain. I repeat things. I hold the same thing up to different lights to see its angles and the qualities of its shadows. I leave some thoughts half-finished. I define and hyperarticulate something small, or take a wildly deep dive into a minor point.

And I frequently can't see the forest for the trees: the whole for the parts, the larger story for the details. That may feel jarring to a reader at times, just as being around an autistic person feels jarring to many neurotypicals. I ask you: Stick with it. Let us teach you how to love us.

That's not to say this book is experimental, only that it may feel a little different at times from more linear memoirs. Julie Brown notes, "[Autistic] writers . . . show a marked resistance against . . . writing . . . [that requires] a sustained, organically whole narrative." She alludes to the work of critic Stuart Murray, who "suggests that the neurotypical notion of narrative may itself be challenged as we become sensitive to the way [autistic people] express their world view through language: [Murray writes that] 'autism may in some way supply narratives of its own, stories and versions of life and its events that differ from those produced within the majority culture.'"[3]

Outside the overall structure of this autistic narrative, my writing can be a bit different at the sentence level too. I'm very particular about language, both in my speech and on the page. In a world of unpunctuated text messages and tweets, of LOLs and emojis, I might come off as annoyingly fussy. The reach for precision in my diction, grammar, and syntax is not stylized—it's an extension of my autistic brain wiring at work.

The Arts and the Relational Sphere

While some of the essays in this book reveal classic signs of autistic brain wiring, others may push back against persistent myths about autistic people. "Autism and Poetry" is a Künstlerroman in miniature, a glimpse at the coming of age of an artist. As I've discovered in the last few years, the very notion of an autistic person steeped in the arts is new to many. We're supposed to be that socially awkward uncle writing code in a dark corner of the basement, or, God forbid, Raymond "Rain Man" Babbitt answering four-digit multiplication problems in milliseconds (notice also: white and male, when the truth is that autism is consistent across cultures and is finally being recognized and diagnosed in women around the globe).

Autistic people are supposed to be immune not only to the creative nuances of the arts but even to art's raw cathartic effects—its very humanity. Indeed, we've had few autistic role models who show us otherwise.

In "Why a Literate Culture Is Important," Thea Temple writes, "The writer's work . . . forces us to see ourselves through others, and, in the process, to 'know thyself.' . . . Literature goes straight to the root of the word 'compassion,' which literally means, 'shared pain.' Sharing another's pain not only heals, but it can prevent injury in the first place."[4]

Self-awareness, especially in the social realm, is not usually associated with autistic people. And sharing peoples' pain—feeling empathy or compassion—has often been thought to be beyond our grasp. In these pages, I aim to reshape that popular narrative and correct misinformation. The truth is, my autistic friends are every bit as—and frequently more—feeling, compassionate, and caring as my neurotypical friends.

I make some of these points about autism, compassion, and the arts in "Diversity and Dignity." In one of the more stunning moments of my career and my life, the mother of an autistic girl wrote to me, thanking me for that short reflection after it had been published. She said, "My daughter is very creative and not drawn to science; she doesn't want to be a Temple Grandin. But she might want to be a Daniel Bowman Jr."

Such an unforgettable remark revealed to me the absence of autistic role models in the arts.

Perhaps near the top of my list of goals for this book, I want to present an alternative vision of autism to a new generation of autistics who will become musicians, painters, poets, novelists, filmmakers, and the like.

The tired notion of us as robots that do not know how to relate must finally be put to rest. I hope I've pushed against that idea in essays like "The Tracks of My Tears," an homage not only to one of my favorite characters in literature but to a group of students I love dearly—and emotionally. Essays such as "Shining like the Sun" also underscore the importance of close, authentic relationships and their centrality to the flourishing of the individual, autistic or not. Though I do not shy away from the challenges of relationship, I also do not underplay its power and significance, and my own deep desire to connect.

Faith on the Spectrum

Of course I speak of autism through personal experience, and Christian faith through the same. They are inextricably connected for me; they have both been with me from the beginning; they are both fraught; filled with shame and anger and the occasional desire to walk away; filled with beauty, truth, and goodness, and the frequent desire to dig deeper; and understood through a glass darkly. I am a product of my time and place, and I claim no particularly supreme knowledge of either autism or Christianity or how they might work best together. What's reflected in this book are signposts from an autistic poet who is a Christ follower, a progressive Episcopalian living in the Midwest, a husband and dad and teacher at a small liberal arts college.

This book doesn't transcend those limitations. It is not a theology of disability soaked in scholarship or biblical hermeneutics; it is not a practical book with tips for helping autistic kids in Sunday school or worship services; it is not a Christian living book providing core "messaging" associated with my "brand." It's a memoir in essays. The word "essay" has an etymology going back to the fourteenth century, and it essentially means to attempt, or to try something out.

. . .

This is my attempt, but at what? Like most memoirs, I suppose it's an attempt to make some sense of my life, a life that still seems strange to me—to weigh some ideas and, more importantly, sensory images, the vivid and specific details of my days. I hope the discoveries I make are useful to you. It's already been transformative for me. I love how writing changes me and makes a little more room for us all. I love how Nell Brown puts it in her essay "This Love":

> I don't want to be penned in by the perceptions of non-autistic people, or by representations that stop at the surface or tell the same story again and again. I want to reclaim space; I want to rest my weight against the boundaries set by others, and push. . . . Writing this is a push, making a little more room for myself and—I hope—others. Can you feel it?[5]

DIVERSITY AND DIGNITY

I like Temple Grandin. And I have a great deal of respect for her trailblazing voice. As a person, an animal scientist, and a writer, she's intense and fascinating, and has done unparalleled work to bring a richer understanding of autism into the mainstream. After actress Claire Danes portrayed her in an excellent biopic in 2010, there was little doubt that Grandin had become the face of the autism spectrum in the US. Although her role in the conversation today is perhaps less prominent than it was a decade ago, her impact is lasting.

Her book *Thinking in Pictures* was among the first own-voices narratives I read, and it taught me a lot about myself and other autistic people. I valued and identified with Grandin's own remarkable story in many ways, and I gained so much understanding from her insights and perceptions.

But the Temple Grandin story is only one story. Like Grandin, I am an autistic professor. And that's about where our similarities end. She is a "prominent proponent for the humane treatment of livestock for slaughter and author of more than 60 scientific papers on animal behavior."[1] Fond of ranches, she's been based in the open air of Colorado for some years now, at a research university.

I teach literature and creative writing at a Christian liberal arts college in corn country.

I know nothing about bovine comportment. I'm allergic to most animals.

Instead, I published a book of poems and recently completed a novel. I'm interested in international poetry, nineteenth-century fiction, big band and early jazz music, Broadway and community theater, the city of London, and the intersection of art and Christian faith.

While I've had moderate success in my career so far, I'm frankly pretty average in my field. And that's exactly why I decided to begin telling my autism story, adding it to the collective understanding of what it means for everyday people on the spectrum. We need to hear from many more autistic voices to begin rounding out the national consciousness of what autism is. We need the voices of autistic scientists and techies and engineers. But we also need to know that the fine arts—poetry, painting, sculpting, music, dance, acting, and more—are not off-limits. In fact, those spaces are often an excellent fit for autistics looking for ways to express and transform both their pain and their joy.

Not long after my diagnosis, I googled "autistic professor." I think I was hoping to find a site where other professors on the spectrum were sharing stories and resources and tips for success in our different academic settings. What I discovered instead is that nine of the ten results on page one were from or about Temple Grandin. The number one alternate search term that the engine suggested to me was "autism cow lady." My heart sank a little.

In her TED talk "The Danger of a Single Story," author Chimamanda Ngozi Adichie reminds us that when just one story comes to stand in for many stories, power is concentrated with the few and the many lose out. She says:

> Power is the ability not just to tell the story of another person, but to make it the definitive story. . . . The single story creates

stereotypes, and the problem with stereotypes is not that they are untrue, but that they are incomplete. . . . The consequence of the single story is this: It robs people of dignity.[2]

The last thing anyone on the spectrum needs is a limited—and limiting—range of images in the public's awareness about what it means to be autistic. While I celebrate any autistic person who has earned acclaim, I also see an urgent need to move beyond a handful of iconic narratives.

So let us continue to add our voices, perspectives, and unique stories. Let us give one another the gift of our diversity, and in doing so, reveal our shared dignity.

SPEAKING THE WORDS

Coming Out as Autistic

It seemed his voice had rusted over. . . . He had never actually said out loud that Ethan was dead. He hadn't needed to: it was in the papers (page three, page five), and then friends had told other friends, and Sarah got on the phone. . . . So somehow he had never spoken the words. How would he do it now?

—Anne Tyler, *The Accidental Tourist*

I am not talking to you now through the medium of custom, conventionalities, nor even of mortal flesh: it is my spirit that addresses your spirit; just as if both had passed through the grave, and we stood at God's feet, equal—as we are!

—Charlotte Brontë, *Jane Eyre*

My first attempt at writing about autism begins with a direct, three-word sentence: "I am autistic."

The simple declaration is the most hard-won line in a piece filled with them. It might be the most hard-won line in all of my writing so far. It opens the gates to a world I've always lived in, a world I'm only just now describing at length . . . a world I hadn't talked about publicly. This last fact has changed, propelling me into new territory. While it was hard enough to write the line, to speak it aloud was even scarier.

I had agreed to present at a gathering of faculty sponsored by my university's Center for Teaching and Learning Excellence, which was curating a series with a more holistic focus: talks by faculty called Identity Intersections. It was a chance to learn about colleagues' lives and careers.

The center fellow was a trusted friend who had read my first autism essay and expressed appreciation; he wanted more of the faculty to hear my story—the beginnings of it, at least. I felt a calling. I knew I had to do it.

And I knew it would be hard. If it were going to happen, I would have to—if you'll permit me the analogy—set aside "customs" and "conventionalities," and perhaps most of all my autistic "mortal flesh," to talk at the level of spirit. Autism is near to the essence of who I am and how I relate to the world, and I would not be able to account for it in any way but with a depth and fullness that transcends everyday conversation.

Oh how that first line, "I am autistic," got stuck in my throat as I stood at the podium and faced my colleagues. I guzzled some water, relaxed my neck and shoulders, spoke low into the mic to help steady my voice. I stumbled my way through a preface.

Then I had no other choice. I said the words. I spoke them with a tremble, as one speaks when ego has been set aside. I stood and talked and kept talking.

Saying the words is an obvious critical step in the process of healing and growth, regardless of the change one has endured. In Anne Tyler's *The Accidental Tourist*, Macon Leary learns that speaking his son's death out loud—even much later, perhaps too late to save his marriage—is the very linchpin of anything resembling recovery. Being a writer and autistic, I've got two good reasons to publish my feelings in print rather than talk them out in a social setting. And yet higher education remains a world of microphones and lectures. Now, I have no problem in the classroom, as it's an environment I mostly control and the content is academic if often personal. Part of teaching is performative, if I'm being honest. But revealing the secrets of my identity that I'm only just beginning to understand . . . that's a different story.

Why was it humiliating? Why did I feel so supremely vulnerable? Let me briefly mention, then set aside, two obvious contributing factors: the very common aversion to public speaking, even among neurotypical people, and the autistic adherence to routine and resistance to change.

Beyond those, my admission was a kind of death: the death of a certain type of image I had wanted to project to the world, to my university, to my family and friends, to myself. I would like to appear intelligent, powerful, accomplished, and self-composed. But I would talk about an inner life filled with fear, with mishandlings of simple social situations, of an abiding loneliness and alienation that has threatened the foundation of my being.

It feels unbecoming for a professor to describe being curled in the fetal position, ritualistically blowing on his knuckles.

Most of us don't want to talk publicly about what hurts, and though autism has had some positive influence in my life, it's also an enormous challenge. Autism is *not* incompatible with personal and professional success, but it complicates the picture. Even as I call for a neurodiversity paradigm, I will not deny that I often experience the autistic life in terms of its negatives.

I feared being misunderstood or being unable to provide good answers to questions. Concepts like neurodiversity are so new that many people, even university professors, may not have encountered them yet. I sensed a disproportionate amount of pressure to educate the audience. And while my talk did contain some exposition, it was mostly personal narrative.

I was not, at that point, ready to accept responsibility for being the resident expert on autism. It's hard to want to share a journey you've barely begun when you can't comment on the big picture, the themes—it's all still unfolding, organic, unpredictable.

Furthermore, and this is upsetting to me and perhaps others, it's possible that I'm scared to accept that responsibility because it is a spectrum, I am every bit as related to the person with lower support needs as I am to the person who needs much greater levels of support than I do—the ones some people historically called the "classic" or "severe" autistic, the developmentally disabled person who may even need full-time care. By virtue of our autism, he is my brother. She is my sister. And I don't really know what that means yet. And I am ashamed of feeling afraid of it. All of this overwhelms me.

. . .

Although I'd like to think this is not true, I may have risked my career by coming forward. Tenure-track professorships are high-stakes affairs—many would like them but few get to have them. To admit to a neurobiological difference may be seen as admitting to a weakness, a professional flaw. I fear planting a seed of doubt: Did he disclose this during the hiring process? Does this affect his teaching?

Of course it affects my teaching, though it's complicated—some facets of autism are problematic while others are strengths. One of Hans Asperger's most frequently quoted lines, for example, is a testament to the obsessive focus typical of people on the spectrum: "It seems that for success in science or art, a dash of autism is essential."[1] This focus mostly makes me better in my roles on campus. It is a gift of neurodiversity.

But would my colleagues entertain darker questions? Questions like: Should his job belong to someone else? Someone better equipped to handle the daily stresses of university life? Especially after reading Steve Silberman's sweeping book *Neuro-Tribes*, I can't ignore centuries of abuse, mistreatment, and a near-complete misunderstanding of autistic people. And one need only read comments on any autism-related social media post to see that (to put it charitably) suspicion about us is alive and well.

These questions hit me in the gut. My university has been very good to me, and I should know better than to indulge these ugly thoughts. But hopelessness creeps in, and it's easy to start thinking that at any moment someone will call me to their office and take away my ability to earn a living and support my family, and that will be that.

But my job is also much more to me—it's a vocation, a calling. I believe in story and I know some things about writing and I love mentoring students. I believe in promoting flourishing through the humanities. I love being an English professor. I overidentify with my career, sometimes equating it with my self-worth. I am terrified of the rug being pulled out from under me for being autistic, and I hope and pray I did not invite such a gesture.

. . .

In the end, by speaking the words, I did what I had to do—if there's fallout to fear, I haven't heard of it yet. In fact I received some very supportive messages from colleagues. Owning this publicly has enabled me to begin a new journey. For one thing, I want to get better at talking about autism so I can do more of it in the future, and the only way to get better is to practice. I was happy to have the first step out of the way.

What's more, I feel empowered. God promises us that his strength is made perfect in our weakness—that if we humble ourselves, he will lift us up. And in front of people whose opinions I value I admitted to being very different and sometimes being unable to manage it and sometimes being humiliated and ashamed of feeling humiliated, and simply uncertain about the whole deal.

For better or worse, this was good soul work.

. . .

A few days later, at my next social gathering, I noticed I was more aware of and in control of my reactions and emotions, a little less afraid, more conscious of expectations and how I might or might not meet them.

I felt a little happy.

I sensed—for the first time in a long while—the palpable joy of being surrounded by friends. I could focus more on them, on their warmth toward me and each other, on the stories they told, on what it means to live in community and to be present.

This is not an indictment of those who choose, for many reasons, not to share their neurodivergence. We must all do what we think best. And don't get me wrong: I did not, and cannot, "overcome" autism—that's not the point either. I'm not sure if I can get "better" at autism, at doing the autistic life. But like anyone else, I can take steps toward wellness—and speaking the words was an important step.

Though my next steps might very well be backward, I pray I'm on the right path.

A PORTRAIT OF
THE AUTIST AS
A YOUNG MAN

YouTuber Gave Up Adopted Chinese Son with Autism after Monetizing Him Online

"I wouldn't trade him for anything!" parenting vlogger Myka Stauffer said about her adoptive son two years ago in a post that doubled as an ad for laundry detergent.

. . . The couple now say that they decided to "rehome" the 4-year-old.

—*Huffington Post*, May 28, 2020[1]

Florida Woman Arrested for Drowning Her Autistic Son after Telling Police Two Black Men Abducted Him

From AP: In an interview Saturday, Miami-Dade State Attorney Katherine Fernandez Rundle said Patricia Ripley apparently tried to drown her son an hour earlier at a different canal but nearby residents heard yelling and rescued him. Then, Fernandez Rundle said, Ripley drove her son to another canal.

"Unfortunately when she took him to the second canal, there was no one there," Fernandez Rundle said.

Fernandez Rundle also noted that because the boy was non-verbal, he could not have told his initial rescuers what had happened with his mother.

"He can't say anything to his rescuers. We talk about children being voiceless. This is another level of voicelessness. He was incapable of saying that 'mommy put me in the water.'"

—*The Root*, May 26, 2020[2]

Dear parent or guardian,

First things first: I know it can be hard, but please don't abandon or murder the autistic kid in your life. Hear me out.

I am an autistic American who has, as of this writing, lived seven years past my life expectancy of thirty-six. The odds were not in my favor. I'm doing okay in life now, though you'll see my first eighteen years were not super promising.

I'm glad no one abandoned or murdered me.

Before you think that the kids in those news reports were likely on the extreme side of things: no. I work with university honors students who didn't speak until age four, or who presented with "challenging" behaviors, including some in the category of "oppositional/defiant," in the face of a complete inability by families to determine and meet their needs.

The kids in these articles could have grown up to be my students—several of whom you'll meet later in this book.

The kids in these articles could have been me. Let me tell you about me, using, for now, the barest outline of events.

I survived my childhood. I got through elementary school even though I did no homework, never studied for quizzes or tests, and almost never spoke with a teacher. Those things confused and scared me. Instead I played or read alone in the backyards of foulmouthed, chain-smoking babysitters whose only interaction with me consisted of calling loudly at noon to come eat a bologna sandwich on spongy store-brand white bread, which I washed down with grape Kool-Aid before disappearing back outside to be alone. I was a master at disappearing.

I walked the halls of my school as if in an extended daydream. When I got home I lit out for the woods or hopped on my bike and rode to the newsstand where I bought penny candy and Spider-Man comic books, or played arcade games like Ms. Pac-Man in the back room.

Adults called me shy and oversensitive, and constantly scolded me for it. I distrusted most of them. They lacked imagination.

As a teenager I had zero interest in the majority of coursework high school offered and would wing it for an overall GPA of about 2.3 out of 4, or a C+. I would be suspended from school for a run-in with the principal, get a tattoo and a motorcycle, shotgun cans of frothy Utica Club and smoke blunts by bonfires on country roads, become the slightly-better-than-average captain of our wrestling team and the decidedly-below-average boyfriend to a string of girls who deserved literally anyone else at all. Even by teenage boy standards, I lacked self-awareness and couldn't possibly imagine what constituted a healthy relationship.

I just didn't get how to do things, how to connect, how to be. I didn't know why it was so hard for me when it was so easy for others.

In the spring of my senior year, I'd meet with a recruiter for the United States Marine Corps who would unceremoniously reject my application for military service because of my asthma. Having worked since I was thirteen for a contractor installing asphalt shingles on roofs in the hottest months of summer, I had a bad taste in my mouth for the only kind of job for which I was qualified.

In a moment of desperation, I visited my high school guidance counselor, a short man with thick glasses and hairy arms. He inspired little confidence yet held the key to my future: a dusty brochure carousel holding trifold pamphlets featuring smiling young people clutching books while walking leaf-strewn paths to Gothic buildings that seemed like they'd make you smart if you weren't already.

I told him I would like to go to a Christian college and asked if he knew any. He looked at me with suspicion. Then he said that Bethany Whittaker had decided on a place called Roberts Wesleyan College in Rochester. Bethany Whittaker was one of the most accomplished members of our graduating class. She was academically in the top ten, was selected all-state in band and choir, had roles in the school plays, and was generally the diametric opposite of me. I thought: if it's good enough for her, I'm sure I'd be lucky to go there.

I would apply to precisely one college, Roberts Wesleyan, and get in on the strength of my application essays alone, a fact that the admissions counselor—and, much more importantly, the financial aid folks—told me in no uncertain terms. And I would happily accept their terms: unthinkably huge loans in numbers that didn't feel remotely real. I had botched relationships with girls and friends and family members so badly at that point that all I wanted was to leave town. I was grateful to head off to Roberts.

(Oh, I should tell you what became of Bethany Whittaker: we've been married for twenty-two years. We both write books and are raising beautiful children in a drafty Victorian in Middle America.)

I had no idea what it would look like to go to college, what I might do there, or how I would live out my days. At age eighteen I knew only two things for sure:

1. All the God stuff I'd grown up with, despite the pain it sometimes caused me and the contradictions I saw, had somehow . . . taken. From baptism, first confession, and confirmation in the Irish-Catholic Blessed Sacrament, to my teen years in a hardcore Catholics-Are-Going-to-Hell (And-So-Are-Most-Others) Baptist church complete with a fundie Bob Jones grad at the pulpit, faith still took root, found a receptive home in my heart. I believed in, and loved, and wanted to follow Jesus of Nazareth. I was a Christian.

2. There were these moments in life that felt better, stronger, more intimate and interesting than others, and they often came through an encounter with art: a book, music, a movie, a play, or, on the rare occasions I saw such things, even a painting or sculpture. There was something so qualitatively different about those moments, and though I couldn't name it, I could feel it, and it felt better than anything. It felt like love—and since God was love, it felt like God.

I took up a major in English at Roberts Wesleyan College. I got by well enough despite unknowingly suffering from autistic executive dysfunction. I lived for those moments when faith and stories came together—both, after all, had to do with what it meant to be a person, what one professor grandly called "the human condition." I was hooked on such talk at once. I wanted to live in those moments forever, quite literally. One way, I thought, to accomplish this would be to get on a career path toward becoming a professor at a Christian college. Then I could get paid to think about the relationship between Christianity and art.

Also, I'd been writing poems. I wanted to be a poet. On the back cover of every poetry collection I read, the author bio said approximately the same thing: So-and-so holds an MFA from such-and-such university; has published poems in these-and-those magazines; and teaches English at such-and-such college. The formula I needed to follow was plain as day: get an MFA, publish poems in journals, and find a university teaching job.

Right out of college I taught high school. This was a good first step for someone who'd grown up disappearing. This was the opposite of disappearing: it was standing in front of a room being in charge of everyone and everything. It was sink or swim. Tenth-grade remedial English students at Indian River Central School would be my teachers until I could, in turn, learn to teach them. And I did.

I went on to write copy for an instructional design firm, where I acquired a better grasp of the power of a good sentence, learned to schmooze with Fortune 500 clients, and figured out lots of techy things that have been useful in my life. I got a fellowship for an MA program in comparative literature at the University of Cincinnati, which allowed me to take creative writing workshops with famous writers; then got an MFA from the low-residency program at Seattle Pacific University (the only program in the country that combined art and faith).

During my MFA, I began adjunct college teaching, then had the chance to take a full-time one-year replacement position in creative writing at Houghton College for a guy on a Fulbright to South Korea. From there I accepted a tenure-track professorship at Taylor University in Indiana.

In fact, the chair of Taylor's English department had to leave a message on my flip phone because I had no reception on the ferryboat from Whidbey Island to Port Townsend, Washington. I was offered an interview for my dream job during my MFA graduation residency. The most conventional mind in Hollywood wouldn't have written such a clean ending.

I have now taught for over a decade. I earned tenure and promotion to associate professor, and will be eligible for promotion to full professor.

My first book of poems, which came out with a small press in Chicago a few years ago, says the stuff about having the MFA, publishing the poetry in magazines, and teaching English at a college. And the last decade of my professional life has been characterized by deep thinking about the relationship between art and Christian faith and, believe it or not, mentoring some of the brightest and most delightful young people I've ever met.

Why do I tell this story in light of the abuse and murder of autistic children? And why do I tell it using only the barest outline of facts?

Because I was lost and now I'm found.

Things started out hard. And things turned out mostly okay. My life as an undiagnosed autistic kid was tough and weird, but I got through it, and I even achieved my dream.

No one "rehomed" or killed me for being autistic, and, despite the challenges, I have done some good things. I'm a decent citizen. I'm thankful for a marvelous life partner and two kids who bless us every day. I'm thankful for a church that edifies and challenges me. And while I don't think that being a professor at a liberal arts college is better than some other outcome, I know it's the one I wanted. And when you talk with parents about their kids' futures, don't they often say, "I just want them to be happy"?

I'm happy. And a lot of other autistic kids would be too if we didn't abandon or murder them (or Other them so intensely that they're driven toward self-harm). Not only might they turn out happy; they might also contribute beautifully to the world—to our lives. To *your* life.

Let us turn the table on these too-common narratives. Let us not just allow these children to live; let us support them so they can flourish.

Yours,
Dan

THE NEURODIVERSITY PARADIGM

An Autism Minor

In the fall of 2019, a group of psychology professors at my university began offering a new minor they'd been developing: autism studies.

The newly conceived path excited me but also had me concerned, as many clinical services and educational resources are formed with no input from autistic people. This would mean they might be operating—and teaching—from a pathology paradigm, calling autism a disorder only and having little access to the complex gifts of neurodiversity and life on the spectrum. And they'd be doing it right next door to where I, an autistic professor, thrive as a writer, teacher, and mentor.

The language surrounding the new minor in the campus newspaper was indeed hurtful to me. I hesitate to throw a student writer under the bus, but the article was . . . unhelpful, to be kind. Of course, no one took notice except one colleague who follows my work and understands some of the dynamics of language surrounding autism.

The student author used phrases like a family "dealing with" a "severe case of autism," as one might deal with a severe case of hives from an allergy. They also positioned it very much in the White Savior and Western missionary tradition, as a "ministry" to "help"—*not* to help autistic people, mind you, but to help their "struggling families"! The negativity, lack of comprehension, and absence of insight stung but didn't surprise me.

The Pathology Model versus the Neurodiversity Paradigm

If you aren't sure that a pathology paradigm is so bad, I want to simply place the language of pathology side by side with the words of a neurodiversity paradigm, and let you put yourself in the shoes of someone on the receiving end of each.

This section will be heavy on quotations from outside sources. I want to stay somewhat out of the way so you can see how the pathology paradigm centers the comfort of the neurotypical while harming the autistic. This viewpoint has been used as an excuse to mistreat and even abuse autistic children and adults time and time again, from institutionalization to applied behavior analysis to bullying and marginalizing.

In an October 2020 article for *ADDitude Magazine*, reviewed by *ADDitude*'s ADHD medical review panel, Janice Rodden offers up the typical language of the pathology paradigm:

Common symptoms of autism in adults include:

- Trouble interpreting facial expressions, body language, or social cues
- Difficulty regulating emotion
- Trouble keeping up a conversation
- Inflection that does not reflect feelings
- Difficulty maintaining the natural give-and-take of a conversation
- Tendency to engage in repetitive or routine behaviors
- Only participates in a restricted range of activities

- Strict consistency to daily routines; outbursts when changes occur[1]

This feels, at the least, like an unnerving suspicion of me and people like me. We have all these "difficulties" and "troubles" and strange "tendencies" and "outbursts." We are weird. We are less than.

I am not whole. I am *unnatural*.

Ironically: notice that many of these items are not at all limited to people on the spectrum! I know plenty of neurotypicals who have "difficulty regulating emotion," but in them, we might call it *passion*—say, the quarterback who pumps his arms and screams when he hits his wide receiver in the end zone on any given Sunday. We admire it; we pay to see emotion . . . as long as it's shown in acceptable neurotypical ways. A word for this is *ableism*.

And how about "only participates in a restricted range of activities"? Does that mean the neurotypical brain is characterized by participation in a wide range of activities? Because I know many people who come home from the same job night after night for decades and do pretty much the same thing: crack open a beer and watch television until bedtime.

. . .

Below is another list, even worse, written for MedicineNet. This is from Dr. Melissa Conrad Stöppler, a US board-certified anatomic pathologist with subspecialty training in the fields of experimental and molecular pathology. Dr. Stöppler is co-editor-in-chief of *Webster's New World Medical Dictionary*. In other words, she's a gatekeeper of language, an influencer with the power to shape the ways people think and talk about autistic lives.

Note that this is the first item that comes up on Google as of this writing when searching for "symptoms of autism." I used the word "symptoms," a term used by those employing a pathology paradigm, rather than the neutral terms "characteristics" or "traits":

Other autism symptoms and signs

- Abnormal Body Posturing or Facial Expressions
- Abnormal Tone of Voice
- Avoidance of Eye Contact or Poor Eye Contact
- Behavioral Disturbances
- Deficits in Language Comprehension
- Delay in Learning to Speak
- Flat or Monotonous Speech
- Inappropriate Social Interaction
- Lack of Empathy
- Lack of Understanding Social Cues
- Not Engaging in Play with Peers
- Preoccupation with Specific Topics
- Problems with Two-Way Conversation
- Repeating Words or Phrases
- Repetitive Movements
- Self-Abusive Behaviors
- Sleep Disturbances
- Social Withdrawal
- Unusual Reactions in Social Settings
- Using Odd Words or Phrases[2]

How do you think it is to be autistic and be described in those ways? To have your everyday traits and habits, which you've been made to feel ashamed of in brutally harmful ways since childhood, described to every Google user around the world as "abnormal," "inappropriate," "lack[ing]," "disturb[ed]," "withdraw[n]," "self-abusive," "poor," and "odd"?

Let me ask you, dear reader: if you've made it this far in my book, if you've invested time and emotional energy in my story to this point . . . do you believe *I'm* disturbed? Inappropriate?

Lacking? To have one's life reduced to a list of synonyms for bizarre, deviant, scary, and out of control . . . think of how that feels and how that translates to the treatment of autistics, perhaps especially those with high support needs.

Can you begin to imagine why the average life expectancy of the autistic is just thirty-six years? Why the suicide rate among autistics is ten times higher than that of the general population?

* * *

Compare the damaging tone and substance of these bullet points to the list of traits of autistic people, written in highly accessible language, by the Autistic Self Advocacy Network (ASAN). Note the emphasis on differences rather than "abnormalities," "troubles," and "outbursts." I want to quote this material at length rather than try to summarize it. It is, in my opinion, the best language we currently have. It's clear, respectful, honest, comprehensive, nuanced, and spectrum-oriented (note the use of "might" and "may" as expressing possibility and probability while also accounting for differences among individuals). It is, indeed, the language I hope professors and students will adopt in autism studies here and at other universities:

> Every autistic person experiences autism differently, but there are some things that many of us have in common.
>
> 1. **We think differently.** We may have very strong interests in things other people don't understand or seem to care about. We might be great problem-solvers, or pay close attention to detail. It might take us longer to think about things. We might have trouble with executive functioning, like figuring out how to start and finish a task, moving on to a new task, or making decisions.
>
>   Routines are important for many autistic people. It can be hard for us to deal with surprises or unexpected changes. When we get overwhelmed, we might not be able

to process our thoughts, feelings, and surroundings, which can make us lose control of our bodies.

2. **We process our senses differently.** We might be extra sensitive to things like bright lights or loud sounds. We might have trouble understanding what we hear or what our senses tell us. We might not notice if we are in pain, or hungry. We might do the same movement over and over again. This is called "stimming," and it helps us regulate our senses. For example, we might rock back and forth, play with our hands, or hum.

3. **We move differently.** We might have trouble with fine motor skills or coordination. It can feel like our minds and bodies are disconnected. It can be hard for us to start or stop moving. Speech can be extra hard because it requires a lot of coordination. We might not be able to control how loud our voices are, or we might not be able to speak at all—even though we can understand what other people say.

4. **We communicate differently.** We might talk using echolalia (repeating things we have heard before), or by scripting out what we want to say. Some autistic people use Augmentative and Alternative Communication (AAC) to communicate. For example, we may communicate by typing on a computer, spelling on a letter board, or pointing to pictures on an iPad. Some people may also communicate with behavior or the way we act. Not every autistic person can talk, but we all have important things to say.

5. **We socialize differently.** Some of us might not understand or follow social rules that non-autistic people made up. We might be more direct than other people. Eye contact might make us uncomfortable. We might have a hard time controlling our body language or facial expressions, which can confuse non-autistic people or make it hard to socialize.

Some of us might not be able to guess how people feel. This doesn't mean we don't care how people feel! We just need people to tell us how they feel so we don't have to guess. Some autistic people are extra sensitive to other people's feelings.

6. **We might need help with daily living.** It can take a lot of energy to live in a society built for non-autistic people. We may not have the energy to do some things in our daily lives. Or, parts of being autistic can make doing those things too hard. We may need help with things like cooking, doing our jobs, or going out. We might be able to do things on our own sometimes, but need help other times. We might need to take more breaks so we can recover our energy.[3]

Realistic, challenging, and centered on the everyday experiences of autistic people (written by us, using "we" rather than "they") instead of on the comfort of allistics: that is the heart of the neurodiversity paradigm.

Just for fun: here's a parody, pointing out the absurdities of centering one group's perceived strengths while pathologizing the typical traits of another. Written by Erik Engdahl, the piece incidentally also debunks the myth that autistic people don't understand humor:

What Is NT Syndrome?

Neurotypical syndrome is a neurobiological disorder characterized by preoccupation with social concerns, delusions of superiority, and obsession with conformity.

Neurotypical individuals assume that their experience of the world is either the only one, or the only correct one. NTs find it difficult to be alone. NTs are often intolerant of minor differences in others. When in groups NTs are socially and behaviorally rigid, and frequently insist upon the performance of dysfunctional, destructive, and even impossible rituals as a way of maintaining group identity. NTs find it difficult to communicate directly, and have a much higher incidence of lying as compared to persons on the autistic spectrum.

How Common Is It?

Tragically, as many as 9,625 out of every 10,000 individuals may be neurotypical.

Are There Any Treatments For NT?

There is no known cure for Neurotypical Syndrome.

However, many NTs have learned to compensate for their disabilities and interact normally with autistic persons.[4]

The send-up still makes me laugh every time.

. . .

Dr. Barry Prizant is one of today's leading autism scholars and has over forty years of experience as a clinical scholar, consultant, researcher, and program consultant to autistic children and adults. He served as a tenured professor of communication disorders at Southern Illinois University and Emerson College, Boston, where he developed specialty tracks in language disabilities and autism in the master's and doctoral programs.

Prizant has led the way in building bridges between the old pathology models and the humane neurodiversity paradigm—helping countless autistic individuals and their families. Notice how he puts it in his book *Uniquely Human*:

> The behavior of [autistic] people isn't random, deviant, or bizarre, as professionals have called it for decades.
>
> Autism isn't an illness. It's a different way of being human. [Autistic] children aren't sick; they are progressing through developmental stages as we all do. To help them, we don't need to change or fix them. We need to work to understand them, and then change what *we* do.
>
> Instead of classifying legitimate, functional behavior as a sign of a pathology, we'll examine it as part of a range of strategies to cope, adapt, communicate and deal with a world that feels overwhelming and frightening. Some of the most popular

autism therapies make it their sole aim to reduce or *eliminate* behaviors.

It's not helpful to dismiss what [autistics] do as "aberrant" or "noncompliant behavior" (a phrase used by many therapists). Instead of dismissing it, it's better to ask: What is motivating it? What purpose does it serve? Does it actually help the person, even though it looks different?[5]

The last analysis of the subject will go, for now, to #OwnVoices autistic scholar Dr. Nick Walker. Walker is associate professor and adjunct senior lecturer at California Institute of Integral Studies in San Francisco. I've found his work profoundly helpful.

The following passages come from an essay by Walker that originally appeared in the 2012 groundbreaking anthology *Loud Hands: Autistic People, Speaking.* Here he touches specifically on the role of language in the paradigm shift, examining the biases implicit in equating autism with illness. Then he considers the futility of the concept of a "normal" or "default" brain or person, drawing an analogy to destructive concepts like a "normal" or "default" ethnicity or culture.

The shift from the pathology paradigm to the neurodiversity paradigm calls for a radical shift in language. If a person has a medical condition, we might say that "she has cancer," or "she suffers from ulcers." But when a person is a member of a minority group, we say "she's Black," or "she's a lesbian." We recognize that it would be outrageously inappropriate—and likely mark us as ignorant or bigoted—if we were to refer to a Black person as "having negroism" or being a "person with negroism," or that someone "suffers from homosexuality."

So if we use phrases like "person with Autism," or "families affected by Autism," we're using . . . language that . . . accepts and reinforces the assumption that Autism is intrinsically a problem.

In the language of the neurodiversity paradigm . . . we speak of Autistics in the same way we would speak of any social minority group: I am Autistic. I am an Autistic. I am an Autistic person.

. . . The concept of a "normal brain" or a "normal person" has no more objective scientific validity—and serves no better purpose—than the concept of a "master race." . . . In the context of human diversity (ethnic, cultural . . . or any other sort), to treat one particular group as the "normal" or default serves to privilege that group.

. . . The concept of "normal" is absurd in the context of racial, ethnic, or cultural diversity.[6]

I hope that we can put to rest the issue of the pathology paradigm—still widely used among medical personnel, therapists, writers, parents, charities, support organizations, and educators—and instead work toward adopting the neurodiversity paradigm.

I pray this happens on my campus and at colleges everywhere.

The neurodiversity paradigm takes into account the complexities of autism, allowing for those of us with both higher and lower overall support needs. It positions us not as freaks to be studied or fixed but as humans, God's beloved, created in his image.

Update from Campus

Since first writing this essay, I've had opportunities to see Taylor's autism minor in action. Autistic students and I have been invited to participate in a number of events, including a talkback session after a film screening; a panel discussion on removing barriers for autistic students (which was well attended by faculty from many disciplines); and several class sessions. Contrary to the worries I'd entertained, I've found that the department, and Dr. Vance Maloney in particular, is sensitive to and aware of our perspectives, actively seeking us for input. They even hired an autistic adjunct professor, my friend and now colleague Haley Moss, an excellent writer, teacher, and the first openly autistic female attorney in the state of Florida. The department is also planning a conference that centers #Own Voices. Though there is still work to be done, I've seen great strides in teaching about autism and autistic people.

 PLACE

COMFORT OBJECT
AND SPECIAL INTEREST

I want to talk about geography as a shaping force, not a subject.
. . . A specific and particular setting for human experience and
endeavor is, indeed, central. . . . I would say a sense of place is
also critical to the development of a sense of morality and of
human identity.

—Barry Lopez, "A Literature of Place"

Reality to an autistic person is a confusing, interacting mass of
events, people, places, sounds and sights. Set routines, times,
particular routes, and rituals all help to get order into an unbearably chaotic life. Trying to keep everything the same re-
duces some of the terrible fear.

—Therese Jolliffe, "Autism: A Personal Account"

LIVING MAPS

Into the Heart of the Heartland

> For each home ground, we need new maps, living maps, stories
> and poems, photographs and paintings, essays and songs. We
> need to know where we are, so that we may dwell in our place
> with a full heart.
>
> —Scott Russell Sanders, "Buckeye"

This morning I reached into my T-shirt drawer in the pitch black.
I didn't want to wake up my wife . . . and I didn't need to. I knew
which shirt I wanted—my plain black Fruit of the Loom—and I
comprehended it by touch. In fact it was underneath two other
T-shirts. I knew them by touch also: my PaoliFest 2019 and my
Utica Blue Sox T-shirt purchased at Herb Philipson's Army &
Navy Surplus store in Herkimer, New York, before it went out
of business. I couldn't tell you the fabric makeup of those shirts;
I just know them by feel.

My favorite T-shirts are comfort objects. Ask any autistic
about their comfort objects and we'll describe a blanket from
infancy to which we clung well into our teens, or a tattered
hoodie, smelly and unrecognizable after decades of wear. (I have

a flannel shirt from 1993.) Autistic author Sarah Kurchak describes this phenomenon in a recent *Vox* article:

> This effort to establish some stability is often reflected in the way we use consumer goods. We might only wear particular pieces of clothing or only eat a limited number of foods—sometimes only when they come in a specific package. We tend to use the same items over and over again until they fall apart, or we lose them.
>
> If there's a disruption in these patterns, the fallout can range from discomfort to potentially life-threatening dietary changes.[1]

My comfort objects make my days and months manageable. But there was one I had to give up when I moved for my job: the northeastern US. No more swimming in Adirondack lakes. No jumping on the Mass Turnpike to visit our friends in Boston, or grabbing the Metro North in Poughkeepsie to Yankee Stadium in the Bronx or Grand Central in midtown Manhattan. No more walks around the soothing streets of my old hometown, where my family has lived for over three hundred years.

What if your very region is a comfort object? How do you walk away from the patterns and routines you cherished? What do you do when you need to move away?

And is it possible to make a new place into a comfort object?

. . .

I sit on my porch swing on North High Street in Hartford City, Indiana, waiting out a lazy shower on the end of a storm. I've learned that a Midwestern spring thunderstorm—the quality of light across the sky, the texture of saturated clouds, the sound the rain makes on the sidewalk—is different from how it happens where I come from. In my native Mohawk Valley, the sky climbs into the hills; it has corners, or pockets. Rain runs down steep slopes into gorges and swells the Barge Canal, the Mohawk River, the creeks whose names have been forgotten. My adult hometown, the city of Rochester, abides by its own natural rhythms as well; you're never unaware of living on the shore of the great lake, Ontario, in the persistent breezes of July or the lake-effect snow squalls of, well, most other months. The summer sky gets hazy as you look toward the shore.

Those are conditions I understand, and I can express what they do and how they feel. I developed a specific language to account for those places, a register of images that emerged from a combination of lifelong observation and autistic instinct. I knew where I was.

But I'm not there anymore. As a northeasterner in the heartland, it's hard to know how to reconcile myself to the soil or the sky.

Take tornado warnings, for example. Each time a funnel touches Indiana ground, I need my neighbors or the TV weather person to explain the difference between a "warning" and an "advisory," and just how many miles per hour does wind normally move, anyway? What's an acceptable range?

What are the rules of engagement for this place? Maybe there's a pamphlet at the chamber of commerce, or a website.

I don't have the basics down yet, much less an authoritative store of earned images and the voice to articulate them with precision and potency. I'm a writer; I need this language. I'm autistic; I need this certainty in my bones. Furthermore, I teach writing, and I'm obligated to foster in my students a deliberate, reflective relationship with their soil, which, for most students, is this place, now our place. Yet I'm still at a loss as I drive from the university in Upland down narrow, flat Route 26, where the sky rolls in at me, corn on one side and soybeans on the other.

I need to let the Midwest inside, and that will take however long it wants to. Growth always does. But I also need to participate in the creation of meaning. I began by asking the question Mary Oliver asks not once but four times, always in italics, in her poem "Ghosts": *"Have you noticed?"*[2]

Even as I began noticing this place and grasping facts, I saw there was a lot more work to be done. I've looked at the geographical map. Now I needed what writer Scott Russell Sanders calls "living maps": "stories and poems, photographs and paintings, essays and songs," because, he continues, "We need to know where we are, so that we may dwell in our place with a full heart."[3] Being autistic makes the imperative uniquely important; to flourish I must feel safe at the gut level.

Somewhere in the Middle of Nowhere

The default in our culture is to see and define the interior of America in terms of absences, like a photographic negative. "It's the middle of nowhere," a student says. "It's a cornfield," one friend said with a wave of his hand when I told him I taught at Taylor University.

We all know that Hollywood sets its serious TV shows and movies in New York, LA, and other major cities, encouraging the perception that those are the only options for one who would seek a life of meaning, especially in the arts. As the Cincinnati hard rock band Greatmodern snarled ironically, "New York stone, California sand: in between, we're all damned!" The Midwest is flyover country, at best a place to leave, like Jim Burden in Willa Cather's *My Ántonia*, or like James Dean turning from Fairmount, Indiana (just down the road from here), to follow his starlit dreams.

It is easy to love New York and LA, or the idea of such places—to project onto them our hopes and aspirations. This seems especially true in a visual culture where a camera shot never lingers more than a split second, jumping and cutting between the sexiest captures, each flicker of the city lights representing possibility. My cornfields and soybeans do not make the final edit in that world.

Yet the student's statement and my friend's words are reductive. The "middle of nowhere" is, by the rules of the game, somewhere. And what is a cornfield, exactly? My poet's instincts tell me that it's infinitely more interesting—connected to our souls—than we might suspect. Maybe I'm rationalizing or romanticizing. But if there's any truth in the notion that beauty will save the world, then I must learn how to see the beauty that is here, and create a bridge from the experience of beauty to language. Simone Weil writes, "Let us love the land of here below, for God has seen fit that it would be difficult yet possible to love."[4] What is rural Indiana if not just that: difficult yet possible to love, seemingly resistant to our efforts?

. . .

I knew that art would be, for me, a portal to safety, and finally to love.

So I took the first steps toward reading the living maps of the Midwest, haphazardly and obsessively, autistically—to acquire language, image, structure, and security. I wanted to learn how to love this place, to start seeing what it would require of me, and to begin shaping new routines and rituals that would soothe my days and nights.

I revisited Sinclair Lewis's Gopher Prairie, Minnesota, following high-spirited Carrie Milford in *Main Street*. I trailed the scoundrel Elmer Gantry around the preaching circuit. I watched Wing Biddlebaum's likely-autistic hands flutter about Winesburg, Ohio. I read Bharati Mukherjee's *Jasmine*, a story that illuminates the upper Midwest through the life of an immigrant suffering a journey that lands her in rural Iowa. I read William Maxwell's keen perceptions of early-twentieth-century Illinois in *So Long, See You Tomorrow*. I went back even further in time to Hamlin Garland's prairie stories in *Main-Travelled Roads*

(1891). The great Alfred Kazin praised that collection, noting, "Was it not in Garland that American farmers first talked like farmers? Was not Garland among the very first to dedicate his career to realism? It is true."[5]

Garland's, Anderson's, and Lewis's turn-of-the-century Midwest was a difficult, artless region of exhausting work, unmerited suffering, blind patriotism, and puritanical fervor. There was some consolation, however, in that stark place. In his essay "Imagining the Midwest," Scott Russell Sanders notes:

> While Midwestern characters, like the writers who create them, often experience the human world as a series of cages, they also feel restored and liberated by contact with the land. In our vagabond culture we have no ready language for this nurturing link between person and place, so we speak of majesty and charm, dignity and fulfillment, a thrill of recognition, applauding poplars and singing forsythia, the trout leaping, the heart hiding in long grass.[6]

The very writers who bitingly denounced Midwestern vices or austerities could also rhapsodize about the land and all that it meant to them, even after they'd lived away for years. That was one of my first clues into the paradox of this place, a paradox that remains relevant.

Scott Sanders would become a powerful guide to thinking about today's Midwest and the Hoosier state we both call home, a place that, culturally and physically, has both changed a great deal in the last hundred years and stayed much the same. In *Writing from the Center*, Sanders evokes the "battered corner of Ohio" where he spent much of his boyhood, the regal red-tailed hawk gliding across the open sky. In the essay "Buckeye," he offers the buckeye tree and its seed as a wholly Midwestern yet transcendent image: its beauty is as subtle and restrained as life in rural Ohio—but it's also poisonous. He talks about how his father knew the folk names of trees rather than the scientific Latin terms, showing us that Midwestern knowledge was traditionally agrarian, privileging personal experience with the land over other forms of knowing.

Yet ironically, I learned this through reading. I soaked up the language, the stories, the sensory images, the particular styles and tones that signify this place and its people and history.

When I was a child, I felt less awkward and unwelcome in the world when I read. The power of books hasn't lessened. I've finally begun feeling that I can write about my life unfolding here.

Chinua Achebe and Writing Place

In "A Literature of Place," Barry Lopez writes about his native California: "the sound of wind in the crowns of eucalyptus trees," the "banks of saffron, mahogany, and scarlet cloud piled above a field of alfalfa at dusk," and "encountering the musk from orange blossoms at the edge of an orchard."

He concludes, "I find the myriad relationships in that universe comforting. They form a 'coherence' of which I once was a part."[7]

Multiply that comfort with coherence by a factor of ten for someone on the spectrum.

One of the most effective "living maps" I've ever read is West African: Chinua Achebe's *Things Fall Apart*. When I teach the novel, I talk about the relationship between personal identity and the literature of a region; I remind students that Achebe's place and culture had never before been written about, in English, by a Nigerian. The portraits of tribal life from Western writers were largely xenophobic descriptions of childlike savages with shadowy, superstitious belief systems and lifestyles.

Achebe had his work cut out for him, to both provide common ground and describe that which was uniquely Igbo. As a native who received a Western education, he was distinctively suited to the job.

I like to read the first few paragraphs of the novel aloud, then stop and ask students how he's doing so far in terms of drawing a living map:

> Okonkwo was well known throughout the nine villages and even beyond. His fame rested on solid personal achievements. As a young man of eighteen he had brought honor to his village by throwing Amalinze the Cat. Amalinze was the great wrestler who for seven years was unbeaten, from Umuofia to Mbaino. He was called the Cat because his back would never touch the earth. It was this man that Okonkwo threw in a fight which the old men agreed was one of the fiercest since the founder of their town engaged a spirit of the wild for seven days and seven nights.
>
> The drums beat and the flutes sang and the spectators held their breath. Amalinze was a wily craftsman, but Okonkwo was as slippery as a fish in water. Every nerve and every muscle stood out on their arms, on their backs and their thighs, and one almost heard them stretching to breaking point. In the end Okonkwo threw the Cat.
>
> That was many years ago, twenty years or more, and during this time Okonkwo's fame had grown like a bush-fire in the harmattan.[8]

When we parse these paragraphs, we see that Achebe nearly redefines an entire continent for a mid-twentieth-century Western reader in fewer than a dozen sentences. He names people and places, inviting non-Africans to reckon with spellings and pronunciations that are so much a part of the life of any region. He shows us a sporting event—an ancient Greco-Roman one at that—that we can identify with, providing common ground. The event includes music, so the identification is even stronger; furthermore, one of the finest athletes is nicknamed "the Cat."

Regions that cheer for teams nicknamed after animals, including the Tigers and the Lions, are invited to relate.

He tells us that Okonkwo's "fame rested on solid personal achievements," demystifying the cultural hierarchy of the tribe and preparing us for some of the more difficult-to-accept tribal practices that will come later in the narrative (such as polygamy). He gives us action that rests on direct conflict, propels the narrative forward, and reveals character.

Then he invents a new West African simile for us to chew on as we adjust to the world of the story: "Okonkwo's fame had grown like a bush-fire in the harmattan." In order to unpack that image responsibly, one may have to research the features of the harmattan and explore the characteristics of a bushfire there, including its aftermath.

All this to say that Achebe has done something extraordinary in his living map: he's shown us that there is as much that connects us with tribal Nigerians as there is that separates us, that Okonkwo is perfectly us and at the same time perfectly Other. World literature happens at the moment each of us in the classroom begins to consider the implications of this tension.

I once showed a poem of mine to a writer from Berkeley, California. His own recent book included poetry set in famous European capitals, complete with italicized phrases in French and Italian. My poem was called "Song to Cincinnati." The older poet couldn't get past the title without a smirk and a comment: "Ha! Funny, some people write about places like that."

I'm sure detractors held similar attitudes about Achebe and the story of his home, questioning the value of writing about a place that had been written off: "In between, we're all damned" indeed.

Nevertheless, some people do write about "places like that." And many more who will never put pen to paper live and die in places like this town where I live right now. They deserve a voice. I don't assume that my Berkeley friend represents the feelings of the majority, but I do wonder if there is still a strong contingency who devalue living in and writing about marginalized places. Maybe a "different kind of citizenship" is in fact needed—is not too radical a concept even today. Maybe in studying our living maps I can know myself, can write from what I'm learning and unlearning, losing and gaining. In the autistic experience, this process is barely a choice; it's a necessity.

Norbert Krapf's Indiana: Familiar Yet Mysterious

Another writer instrumental in my new citizenship has been Norbert Krapf. Like Achebe's, Krapf's work often contains the names of towns and bodies of water and bridges, only his are located in the Hoosier state, from the Mississinewa and Wabash Rivers to James Whitcomb Riley to Jasper, Indiana.

In his preface to *Bloodroot*, Krapf says that the poems "articulate [his] major allegiances": "*Bloodroot* brings together poems rooted in my native place that engage the details of the natural and human history—the external and internal cosmos—of the landscape." He goes on to call Indiana his "familiar yet mysterious universe to explore."[9]

When I came upon the collection, I saw that my instincts would be affirmed: that living "in the middle of nowhere" was in fact living somewhere—somewhere "familiar yet mysterious." Krapf's poems helped me acquire the images and language I crave.

Krapf sometimes works in broad, expansive images that still exude intimacy and appreciation of Indiana. I've found that the poet's skill and restraint, rendered in plain speech, highlight dimensions of place that feel at once traditional and perfectly alive today.

In "God's Country," the immediacy becomes poignant in the combination of sensory images: "onions have / lain down in bacon drippings / in the iron skillet and made / friends with potatoes boiled / in their jackets, sliced into / thin white coins of the realm."[10] The economy of a place is told through details that enable the reader to see, smell, hear, and, at the same time, perceive the larger significance of the scene. While the camera pans, we come to understand the fullness of these establishing shots, the richness of the oeuvre. And we suddenly know this place more robustly, its familiar aspects inextricably linked to its mystery.

Krapf also brings the camera in for close-ups, even extreme ones that capture the minutest—and sometimes most telling—details:

Hauling Hay

As the sun burned
on the back
of your neck
you grabbed a bale
with both hands
by the binder twine
heaved it high
enough to clear
the mounting stack
on the back
of the wagon
pulled along
by a tractor
groaning in low

someone stacked
it just right so
the whole load
somehow held
in balance

and the chaff
swirling in hot
air like a swarm
of sweat bees

settled on your
shoulder, slipped
beneath the collar
of your sweat-
sopped shirt

and pricked
the skin stretched
across your spine.[11]

The story of the poem is simple, so the use of the intimate second-person point of view becomes powerful. Krapf matches form to content by stripping away all but the most spare and terse language, allowing a maximum of two syllables per word but using mostly one-syllable words where one will do. Likewise, no line in the poem contains more than four syllables, and most contain only three. The omission of internal punctuation creates a sense of the whole in each of its parts and establishes the careful rhythm through the repetition of foundational sounds, through rhymes and slant rhymes. The precise construction of the words on the page mirrors the wagon load that, we are told, "someone stacked . . . / just right." The speaker seems to be "groaning in low" like the tractor, doing the work of the poem with Midwestern efficiency.

The prick of the chaff—the most ordinary experience—becomes climactic here, waking us out of our comfort as we sit with the poem and inhabit the image. The chaff and its impact register on the smallest of scales, like the tiny shock of recognition we feel as we discover that a whole world, a whole state, a whole heartland swirls in the air of the poem like when, as a child at Christmas, you picked up a snow globe and shook it.

I taught "Hauling Hay" at the Indiana Writers Center. I read the poem aloud, and as I finished—before I asked a single question—an elderly man raised a shaky hand and simply said, "I know that. That was . . . my life."

. . .

I don't farm, but I live among farmers. I don't harvest the fields, but I drive by them every day. I see and consider them; they are becoming "the furniture of the mind."[12] As are other Indiana images: I go to the Muncie Civic Theatre for a show; I eat at a new fusion bistro in Indianapolis; I attend church with my friends at Gethsemane parish in Marion. I sit on my porch in Hartford City and watch a storm come and go.

I know where I am as these routines transition from special interests—obsessive pursuits borne of fear—to familiar comfort objects, calming my body and mind.

I read the poems of Karen Kovacik and Norbert Krapf, read Susan Neville's essays and Cathy Day's fiction, meditate on the metaphors of Scott Russell Sanders. I hear their words hanging in the air even as I hear the words of my neighbors at the grocery or hardware store. I learn to be in community with all these voices, oriented and thriving in my new world through living maps.

I drive down Route 26 from Hartford City to Taylor University in Upland, the sky rolling in at me, corn on one side and soybeans on the other.

AUTISTIC CULTURE MAKING

> Without honoring any gods, a piece of domestic architecture, no
> less than a mosque or a chapel, can assist us in the commemo-
> ration of our genuine selves. . . . We value certain buildings for
> their ability to rebalance our misshapen natures and encour-
> age emotions which our predominant commitments force us
> to sacrifice.
>
> —Alain de Botton, *The Architecture of Happiness*

The abandoned storefront in the "old downtown": Is there a
more symbolic sight in Rust Belt cities? The buildings sit empty,
windows high above the street boarded up. Those with imagination lament how the intricate turn-of-the-century architecture
is being wasted, that it's probably too late to save it.

We say things like, "If I had the money, I'd turn the down-
stairs into a coffee shop and make loft apartments above." Yet
year after year, they crumble a little more.

That's the scene here in Hartford City. There's a newer business district on Route 3 featuring the usual suspects: abundant
parking spots in front of a grocery store, CVS, McDonald's,

Save-a-Lot. KFC/Taco Bell across the street. It's like that same stretch of businesses in a thousand other towns.

But the old downtown is unique, charming for those with eyes to see. Centered on one of the more fantastic courthouses in the state of Indiana are those storefronts, a few of which house functioning businesses—a hardware store, dry cleaner, furniture store, bank, new computer repair place, even a coffee shop.

I say a prayer for the success of those places when I drive or walk by. We can't afford to lose another one. Lord, help them develop smart business plans. Or, give me the patience to try them before running to the box stores.

If "architecture is frozen music," as Goethe wrote, then beautiful architecture left for dead is doubly frozen. What if we can unfreeze it? Maybe, somehow, we can reclaim one of these buildings, rescue the power of its design and history and integrity—reshape it so it can, eventually, reshape us.

* * *

A few years back, Andy Crouch visited the university where I teach. People around campus had read his first book, *Culture Making*, and some of us were chatting about it. I had first met Andy at the Glen Workshop in Santa Fe, New Mexico. I read *Culture Making* after that meeting, then taught from it in several classes.

As I became steeped in the ideas of the book, I began to believe that I wanted not just to critique or consume culture but rather to *make* culture. I committed to applying those principles to my writing. I focused, for example, not on criticism of others' work, or frantic consumption of books and ideas, but on carefully building my own narratives, improving my craft.

And I've been on a parallel quest for self-improvement—and ultimately to make culture—as an autistic person. I've studied and reflected in counseling to learn the strengths of neuro-divergence, along with facing the challenges of autism. I've read #OwnVoices memoirs like John Elder Robison's *Look Me in the Eye*, Laura James's *Odd Girl Out: My Extraordinary Autistic Life*, Anand Prahlad's *The Secret Life of a Black Aspie*, Katherine May's *The Electricity of Every Living Thing: One Woman's Walk with Asperger's*, and Rees Finlay's unique graphic novel, *Reaffirmation: Coming to Terms with an Autism Diagnosis*. I've devoured coming-of-age fiction by autistic writers, like Sally Pla's *The Someday Birds*, *Rogue* by Lyn Miller-Lachmann, and several wild sci-fi novels by Corinne Duyvis.

I believe in strengthening the architecture and artfulness of the self. Yet when I looked around my little Indiana town, I saw the need to make culture in the public square. I'd never stayed anywhere long enough to try it, but with a tenure-track professorship and our first house, it seemed we were staying put. Seeing those storefronts in Hartford City made me wonder if this was the time to make something that would last beyond me. To put theory into practice where I live would take imagination, hope, hard work, and autistic self-awareness.

Autism and the Arts Center

My chance came when I saw a Facebook post looking for volunteers to help clean out "the old Hallmark store" on Washington Street. A recently formed group called Blackford County Arts had—through a series of generous donations, strategic partnerships, and hopeful volunteers—acquired one of the storefronts and was in the early stages of renovating it.

Better yet, they were going to turn it into an arts center, with programming and instruction for adults and children in music, painting, pottery, and creative writing.

Without a second thought, I got in touch with the group and said, "I'm in."

. . .

I'm glad I spoke up hastily, because I might have backed out had I considered the very real complications autism would present. What if the next workday came when I was emotionally spent from teaching and desperately needed downtime? It's easy to say "Skip one day; it's no problem," but this group had already put in dozens of volunteer hours before I'd even heard about it, and if I were to become part of the team—to make culture—I would, as usual, have to earn my keep on neurotypical terms.

Also: I've spent a lot of my life in classrooms and the hallways of academia. I know the people on campus, and our contexts, intimately. I know, in general, what people are going to do or say in most situations. There's an appealing predictability. Interacting with the folks at Blackford County Arts—a graphic designer, a nurse, a retired state senator, an attorney at law, and an administrator focused on fundraising—was a crapshoot. I would have to work out who they were, how they interacted with one another, what they thought about the world, what they thought about me, all from scratch.

This is simply too much for many of us on the spectrum. We do not have the neurotypical's relational intuition to guide us. Instead we use intellect to hypothesize and test our ideas about people. We often listen for a very long time before speaking (this makes Midwesterners uncomfortable). We try to figure out what people want and sometimes imitate the general tone of things to fit in or "mask." These emotional and mental efforts are exhausting and produce wild spikes of anxiety.

Top that off with the facts of renovation: someone's running a power sander three feet away while another is thwacking at a wall with a pneumatic nail gun and a dump truck's back-up beeper blasts in from the alleyway and the sweat from your brow drips into your eyes as you wipe at it with filthy hands . . . and you have arrived at the Autistic Crossroads—a sensory dilemma screwing with your good-faith efforts at building community.

Cue the guilt and shame that says, *You aren't made for this world. There's no place for you here, and you are less-than for not being able to make this work. It's your fault.*

And if you view, as I do, making culture in your community as an act of your Christian faith; if you see the development of a safe, inspiring environment where all are welcome to cultivate the fruits of the spirit as expressed in the arts as an act of spiritual discipleship . . . well then the voice becomes more ominous: *If you were a better Christian, you would do it. Take up your cross. You're selfish. Lazy. Worthless. You're not contributing. You're not serving. Do you even love your neighbor?*

Much of my life has been plagued by that devil voice, the declarations of internalized ableism—conflating standard neurotypical social behavior with Christian service. And feeling self-hatred because I often wasn't up to it.

. . .

But when I said yes to Blackford County Arts, I didn't think through any of that. I simply showed up and met everyone in my typically quiet, awkward way. We donned dust masks and hauled trash for hours without much fanfare. There was something I really liked about these people. They laughed and joked with one another as they worked and I stayed a step behind, observing while contributing. Some brought bottled water; others ordered pizzas. We ate, then worked some more. The physical labor provided a soothing rhythm, a kind of socially acceptable stimming, and an excuse for not having to chat idly very much at all. I thanked God for such graces.

Over many such Saturday mornings, and dozens of dumpsters, dump trucks, flatbeds, carloads, and recycling bags, we completed step one of the renovation: get rid of the many years' worth of garbage that had filled the building. With each new load of trash removed, the possibility we had dwelled in, that fueled us all, began to look more like a reality.

One of the phrases I learned from Gregory Wolfe's essay in *Image* journal comes from a passage by critic R. P. Blackmur. Blackmur talked about poetry that "not only expresses the matter in hand but adds to the stock of available reality."[1]

In making the arts center, we would add tangibly to the stock of reality available to the citizens of one of the poorest counties in the state. And the particular reality we'd bring would be infused with shalom, a wholeness and harmony, appealing through the arts to the best in us.

Closing In

As we continued gutting the interior of the building, we discovered that the early-twentieth-century pressed-tin ceiling, hidden for all these years high above a tiled drop ceiling, was in serviceable shape. It would take only minor repairs to restore this ornately designed feature, twenty-plus feet above the floor, to something like its former glory. This was a thrilling development.

As efforts continued, I was asked if I would like to serve on the board of directors. The group liked that I was young(ish), had come to nearly all the workdays, and taught at the university in the next town over. I accepted the invitation. It felt so good to be wanted, to be valued in a world that often left me out. We met frequently to plan next steps.

We would hit some road bumps in timing, funding, personnel, and partnerships. The renovation efforts slowed to a crawl for a while, and the building sat at that halfway stage for longer than we wanted.

But we kept chipping away.

. . .

A group of local pastors had come together from various denominations and completed a critical task: drywalling. This allowed us to paint. A two-tub industrial sink was installed. It was hard to walk by it and not picture kids washing their paintbrushes at the end of a Saturday morning class or scrubbing the clay off their hands after making pottery. Possibility abounded again. We would make culture.

A bulkhead, which would contain the new heating system, was constructed around the perimeter of the room. It would also function as an anchor for a gallery hanging system, donated and installed by the local chapter of the Rotary Club. A piano lab was already set up in the back corner of the room; music lessons had begun amid the drywall dust and continuing construction.

We were now at the point where the building clearly would be completed. We would get to solicit the next round of donations with the news that it would go directly toward arts programming.

Tragedy

As the contractors created new debris, we set up a final workday on a Saturday in mid-December for volunteers to clean. The night before, many of our friends had gone to Indianapolis for the Sufjan Stevens Christmas show. We agreed to babysit their kids.

We were planning a quiet evening. Then we heard the news: there had been a devastating shooting—at an elementary school.

We babysat, keeping our own small children and our friends' kids very close that night. Neither Beth nor I got much sleep.

. . .

The next morning, I went to the arts center. I worked hard, not saying a word to anyone. Within minutes, I was dripping sweat, thankful for the mindless work of separating burnable wood from trash and recyclable metal, and loading the garbage into a pickup truck. My body was on autopilot and my mind was numb.

By the time we were done, the building was nearly empty. It was eerily quiet as we got ready to leave. Though not complete yet, the space had been transformed, and I'd been given an inside look.

I stared for a moment at the floor that would soon be replaced by beautiful hardwood and tread on by the feet of children and teachers and community members; the bare walls that would be covered with their art; the pressed-tin ceiling that would inspire with its lavish detail and hold the handsome lights we'd ordered.

· · ·

In the days after the shooting, many would debate gun control, increased security in schools, and mental health care awareness. But I couldn't help thinking that this work was, for me, the most appropriate reaction to that tragedy and other (too-frequent) murders. I saw the arts center with a new urgency: not just as a renovated storefront but as a place where people could come and create, make culture—and make friends—in a world that needed more than ever these safe spaces. It would be one strategy against isolation and anger, a place made for the appropriate expression of those emotions, a place that might finally have the power to, as Alain de Botton says, "rebalance our misshapen natures."

That knowledge helped me keep going even when it got tough. When I sat in our board meetings after a long day at work, when I heard that the contractors had run into some unforeseen problem, or that we were out of money (we were usually out of money), I thought: It doesn't matter. We have to do this. We need this place, and we cannot give up.

Open, and Closed, Doors

We indeed held our grand opening and dedication, and it was by all accounts a success. Our neighborhood came together to celebrate the milestone, knowing too that much more work would need to be done in the coming months and years to sustain the vision.

. . .

My part of the story is a little less happily-ever-after. I'd been through many hours of volunteering, both in the renovation process and as a member of the board. I'd worked long days, and nights, on campus, and the semester showed no signs of letting up.

One day in late winter, I'd been grading and teaching since the break of dawn, attended more meetings than I cared for, had some writing deadlines hanging over my head, skipped lunch to meet with advisees, and got home ten minutes before a board meeting was to begin. My sensory world and emotional energy was in shambles. And the purpose of the night's board meeting? Phone banking. Calling strangers to ask for money.

I remember saying out loud, "I can't do this," and feeling very trapped. All I wanted, all I needed on God's earth, was to swap out my suit jacket and starchy button-down for pajama pants and my favorite raggedy twenty-year-old T-shirt with the name of a long-forgotten beer-league softball team from back home barely visible on the tattered fabric. Nothing else mattered.

I opened up my laptop and wrote an impetuous email: my sudden resignation from the board.

Later, I'd learn the concept of "catastrophizing," of believing you're in a worse situation than you really are. Since many of us on the spectrum struggle to see the forest for the trees, we sometimes fall victim to this form of self-sabotage. It can make for a rather jagged two-steps-forward-one-step-back dance that feels like failure.

A good Hoosier, a good Midwestern man, would have shown up to the meeting, and if he wanted to resign, he would have stood up, looked 'em in the eye, shaken hands with everyone, made all the appropriate thank-yous, and offered, of course, to stay for several more weeks until a suitable replacement could be found. I didn't have it in me. And it's not that I was wrong. Or right. It's that I was different. I am different. I'm autistic.

Making culture, for me, will never look like it does for others. Each time I step out to work in the community, I must find a new way forward, a third way between what they do and what I would do in my worst moment, between overextending myself and simply slinking away. I must silence the voice that equates a nontraditional, autistic approach with a bad take, a half-hearted attempt, or an un-Christian pursuit. I must pray for strength, and also for inner peace: the same peace I pray the people in my town will know when they visit the arts center.

I think often of Ephesians 2:8–9, and wonder if it could be a sort of life verse for autistics: "For it is by grace you have been saved, through faith—and this is not from yourselves, it is the gift of God—not by works, so that no one can boast."

Not by works.

This is truly good news—gospel—for those of us on the spectrum, whose works can often be uneven. Others may be tempted to rest on their achievements, but we autistics are as likely to screw everything up as to produce a great outcome. Or sometimes we do both at the same time. No matter—our grace through faith is a gift, not from ourselves or the result of our works. This opens the door to do things according to the way our brains were made, according to, as the next verse says, "God's handiwork." We too can make culture.

Culture making requires all of us to pitch in however we can. But it can work, and when it does a new reality emerges.

The architecture, the people (both the regular types and the neurodivergent), the art we're making, the art that's making us—each distinct element converges, and we can dwell in possibility together, even those of us on the spectrum, when we open the doors.

RIDING WHILE AUTISTIC

Sitting in an automobile, we see the world as if it were on a television screen. Outside exists on the other side of the glass . . . a slightly unreal world that doesn't conform to our controlled environment inside. It's like watching a newscast from some foreign land, something vaguely worrisome, but that doesn't quite touch us. . . . On a motorcycle . . . we are vulnerable . . . to both the physical and emotional realities of the world. We ride *in* the world, never merely past it.

—Ian Chadwick, "Riding Is More Real"

I shift into my bike's fourth and final gear when the speed limit increases to 55 miles per hour. Opening the throttle with leather-gloved fingers, I watch in my peripheral as the tachometer's tiny hand edges toward the RPM red zone. The internet said this make and model should top out at 77, but now that the engine is forty-five years old, the number feels closer to 70. I don't mind. I'm no adrenaline junkie on a sleek new sport bike. Neither am I planning a cross-country trek on a Gold Wing with overstuffed saddlebags and a tow-behind. I'm a guy with a seven-mile commute down a country road in central Indiana, and my '75 Honda CB200 suits this purpose beautifully.

Row upon row of corn husks push toward open sky. The bean fields have turned a bright maize with shades of saffron. To my left, boughs hang heavy with ripe Osage oranges, which are of course not orange but pale lime, popping to a near-chartreuse against the afternoon sun. The oddly textured spheres look like a compact model of the human brain, or a head of broccoli seen from above. A squirrel darts to a fallen fruit, forages for seeds.

A train track cuts diagonally across the road. I like to be in second gear for the bump; about fifty yards out, I brake the rear wheel gently with my right foot, squeeze the clutch with my left hand, and shift down with my left toes. Back before they paved the crossing I developed a habit of rising off my seat slightly, bearing down on the pegs and absorbing the shock with my knees to keep the bike steady. Though the bump is smoother now, I retain this practice, partly out of reluctance to accept change and partly because I like what it signifies: that as I ride I must make vigilant, subtle physical negotiations with the terrain. That my body and mind participate together. That I am vulnerable. I ride in the world, never merely past it.

Shortly beyond the tracks, an S-curve requires some management. I slow down and lean decisively to the left for one, two, three seconds, then to the right for the same. I use the inner third of the lane first, then hug the curve. Then there's an agreeable rolling hill where I give the gas a quarter-turn just to hold speed. It's often here that I'm at my most defensive: twice this year a car has come headlong and oblivious, the driver looking down at a phone. What is for them a small steering correction is for me a scare that carries nothing less than the weight of death.

Around the bend, the trees form a natural canopy overhead. It's an unusual feature, reminding me more of my upstate New York childhood in the foothills of the Adirondacks than the largely treeless Indiana farm country. The tunnel shades the road. I begin to smell the small bog coming up on the right, hear bullfrogs croaking even over the hum of the engine. A turkey vulture soars low, its wings holding steady in that distinctive slight V. I wonder what carrion has garnered its focus.

I catch sight of the small horse ranch. A mottled white creature stands tall and still in the pasture. I believe they said it was an Andalusian gelding. Some years ago while visiting a church, we met the folks who own this place. It was hard to say no when they insisted we stop at their house to show the kids the horses. Our daughter had been devouring every volume of those ubiquitous "young girl and her horse" books, and our son was game for anything to do with live animals. Our church life picked up elsewhere, and I've never seen the couple since. But when I ride by, I think of them.

The ranch comprises the only landmark on my ride that is peopled. I like it that way. I don't want to know or think about many people on this route. I want to be alone, present to each moment, to the landscape and its exigencies. For within seconds I'll be in town, the small village where my university's sensible brick buildings sprawl across green acres; where being in community with upwards of a thousand people represents unique challenges for an autistic person—challenges that, as life-giving as they are, I can handle for only so long before I need to retreat into solitude again.

· · ·

Most autistic people use various forms of self-regulation, or stimming, such as gentle rocking or feeling certain textures, to calm ourselves. In an interview with the BBC, an autistic woman said that "dribbling sand through her fingers was a feeling that calmed" her, adding that stimming "may counteract an overwhelming sensory environment, or alleviate the high levels of internal anxiety [autistics] typically feel every day." She concluded that stimming helps us "refocus and realign [our] systems."[1] I covet my motorcycle ride as a form of stimulation that benefits me, lowers my anxiety, and helps me better handle my daily tasks and relationships.

Beyond simple stimming, though, the trip down the marsh road enables me to enact a metaphor for the autistic life. Autistic people, like motorcyclists, live deeply in the world; we never merely move past it. I'm talking here about sensory overload, which is common among those of us on the spectrum. It's tougher than people think, that phrase which gets bandied about carelessly in reference to a movie's fast-paced chase scene or the varied smells of a good dinner.

Without getting too far into the specifics of diagnostic types of sensory processing disorders, suffice it to say that many autistic people feel things more sharply and directly, and therefore may respond dramatically to everyday sensory input that would have little or no impact on others. I don't think it's a stretch to claim that it's like the difference between riding a motorcycle and driving a car.

I can be thrown completely off track by visual stimuli such as a sink full of dishes—the urge to wash, dry, and put away everything in the kitchen overwhelms me. If I hear someone sing a fraction of a note off key, I can experience it like nails on a chalkboard; I may need to leave the room and take time to recover. If someone confronts me without warning, I will be startled and upset for several hours. If I'm outdoors and the sun creeps into my shade, I'll need to move immediately or I might have a panic attack and go into full-on meltdown.

The list goes on—and on and on, and varies for every person on the spectrum. We are highly vulnerable in this way. Sensory triggers can feel like an endless stream of challenges created for the express purpose of ruining our days, especially when they come in the context of a social-relational realm that is frequently perplexing, frustrating, and energy sapping. Count your blessings if, like a driver tucked safely inside a comfortable

SUV, you can take much of the world in stride. Most autistic people cannot. We feel every bump, every tiny pebble in the road that threatens a crash.

* * *

The sensory overload I experience on the motorcycle ride down the marsh road is powerful, but it is also soothing, as it occurs within a (mostly) predictable environment that I must honor and engage carefully. In that setting, I can attain success, a concept that often eludes me in many aspects of my life. Both the structure and the work of the ride are comforting.

The clutch and gearshift and throttle and brakes and kick starter—even something as small as a turn signal—do not respond with the fluid grace of a contemporary machine; it's more like driving a vintage car with no power steering. It takes both hands, both feet, and, among other things, a keen vision switching purposefully between straight ahead, left and right, down at the pavement, in both rearview mirrors, to a quickly clouding sky, and across multiple gauges on the bike. Insects from tiny bugs to plump bumblebees hit you in the chest and the head while the incessant gusting of the wind, too, demands to be taken into account at every moment.

Operating the bike in this robust atmosphere takes concerted effort, an effort I've learned through practice. The experience produces a unique serenity for me. I may not be able to control or handle some of what comes my way on an average day, but I can navigate the old marsh road just fine and have fun doing it. That feels good.

And I think it probably spills over into other areas in ways I don't understand. In the autistic life, wins can be tough to come by. So I'll take one wherever I can get it.

COMMUNITY, WORSHIP, AND SERVICE

I will walk among you and be your God, and you will be my people.

—Leviticus 26:12

AUTISM AND CHURCH

There's nothing I love more than a ritual—except maybe a routine. The safety of rituals and routines cannot be overstated. Through establishing a pattern, I can relax. It's coffee at the cafe I know well, or dinner and drinks at your house, or going to the movies. . . . Whatever. Every autistic person is different, obviously, yet in my world I know that there will be no "popping over for tea" unannounced, or insisting that we go somewhere else just as we've sat down, or throwing unexpected guests into the mix.

—Madeleine Ryan, "I'm Autistic,
Here's How to Be Friends with Me"

Coffee hour after the service. Strangers smile wide, pump my hand, ask classic small-talk questions that should be simple but aren't for me:

"How are you?"

I don't know, and I'm not sure if they want a real answer. I tend to take things literally, overthink these exchanges. Would they like me to be real—would it reflect better on who we are as a body of believers if I get honest? Because frankly, I'm often not okay.

Or should I pretend everything's fine like most people do with strangers? If it were me visiting a church, I'd be put off if I got an inauthentic vibe. Then again, I'd be put off if it seemed like they were trying too hard. (I once visited a church where people spoke in the worst evangelical clichés, then thanked one another for being "so transparent.")

I feel the sweat on my forehead; I slurp my coffee too quickly, burning my tongue.

The pastor suddenly issues a call to fill the front of the sanctuary, after I've carefully selected the exact seat I need (near the middle, on the aisle): "Don't be shy, everyone move up—yes, that means you! Plenty of good seats up here!" There's unwanted direct eye contact. I'm frozen with fear.

We're doing "popcorn prayer" in my small group, and although they say you can "pray as you feel led," the expectation is very clear: everyone in the group will pray. I'm the only one who hasn't offered up a petition because my selective mutism has decided to kick in; or my senses are overloaded from the worship band's volume and intensity; or I'm practicing in my head what to say but I'm nervous and know the words won't come out right; or I'm afraid that my concerns—the confessions and petitions I want to offer up—are so markedly different from those I've just heard that I'd better keep it simple.

Anyone got a sick grandma? That's an easy one. Please toss me a softball and mention your sick grandma.

Someone behind me touches me with no warning and begins praying into my ear. Their breath tingles my skin, which I'd crawl out of if I could. Others lay their hands on my highly sensitive neck, shoulders, and head, startling me, making me cringe . . . making me wish I'd stayed home this morning.

———

My first experience in a community of belief took place in upstate New York, where I was baptized, confirmed, and communed in the Catholic Church. The journey into Protestant faith has been circuitous, including worship in Baptist, Presbyterian, Free Methodist, Vineyard, and various nondenominational traditions. My wife and I have always tried to find a church that suited us in terms of our growing understanding of God and our family needs. Sometimes that meant no church at all. Plus we moved around a lot, so we landed in many different settings.

The vignettes above occurred in good churches, formative houses of worship for me. Before I had an autism diagnosis, of course, I couldn't put my finger on why those scenarios—"popcorn prayer" or other instances of unrehearsed spontaneity, being asked to move seats—made me so uncomfortable. I assumed I was just painfully introverted, shy, fretful, perhaps just temperamentally unsuited for church. I followed Jesus but never quite felt at home in a congregation. Not many others seemed to clam up when the pastor said, out of the blue, "Now turn to your neighbor and look him in the eye and say, 'God loves you!' Now give him a hug!"

Why couldn't I just roll with it?

Did I lack trust in God? Did I lack the Holy Spirit? Was I not fit as a member of the body of Christ?

I wrestled with these issues, and the shame they brought, for years. Only in recent years did I begin working through them with a better knowledge of who God made me to be, and what I need to thrive.

Like most people on the spectrum, I need some structure and predictability. Surprises are challenging. Unwanted physical exchanges can be difficult. I often can't sustain eye contact, and shouldn't have to. Some weeks, I'm overloaded and simply cannot participate in activities that fall in the category of fellowship; therefore, my church attendance is spotty. Among the many things church is, it's a complex, multilayered social environment, a gauntlet of unspoken rules and expectations requiring vigilant navigation. If it's already been a long week, I may need a Sabbath that includes much more rest and time away from all people—including staying home from church.

"I would never have known; you don't look autistic."

"Are you sure you have autism? You just need to learn to relax—smile, life's not that bad. God is in control!"

"My nephew has autism and you're not like him at all. You're really high-functioning."

"I think you mean 'a *person* with autism.' Saying 'autistic' is offensive."

"It's inspiring that you're overcoming your autism. You can beat this! You can do all things through Christ."

"Well, I guess we're all a little autistic, right?"

Now that some people in my faith circles know I'm autistic, it can be frustrating to communicate the nuances of what that means. People often say things that are hurtful or reductive, or simply betray a lack of understanding. The comments above are not hypothetical, or anomalous—I've heard them all. I sometimes feel like I've been dubbed Ambassador of the Autistic Community, that I'm supposed to model healthy autism and the integration of autism and faith, gently teaching anyone who's interested. That's a lot of pressure when my emotional energy is consistently near-drained. And yet I still feel traces of shame for not being up to the task.

Since my diagnosis, I know I don't have to feel ashamed anymore. And that's perhaps the key takeaway I'd like to offer to fellow Christ followers: as you live and worship alongside your autistic neighbors, you can help free us from the shame we've carried. No one expects you to walk on eggshells or get everything right. Just aim for greater knowledge and empathy. Listening to our stories—including reading books like this—is a great start.

. . .

These days my family and I attend an Episcopal church. We have friends there, which helps put me at ease. And the Episcopal rites feature marvelous predictability through liturgy, tradition, and a year-round calendar of meaningful and structured holy days. I know what to expect, and I find richness in it, whether it's responsive Scripture reading; the Book of Common Prayer; the sung liturgy (a call and response led by our priest); or the taste of the cold steel chalice and the tang of warm red wine on my lips as I kneel at the communion rail. It all works for me.

This is not to say there will always be a direct relationship between autism and "high church" settings. The aphorism from autistic circles bears repeating in the context of faith: "If you've met one autistic person . . . you've met one autistic person." While we share a constellation of traits to various degrees, people on the spectrum are unique individuals who land in many denominations and churches.

Ministers and congregants: you may not know it, but we're in *your* church.

I pray that your minds and hearts are open to us. For we too are fearfully and wonderfully—if a little differently—made.

SHINING LIKE THE SUN
Antler and Authentic Christian Community

On March 18, 1958, a Trappist monk named Brother Louis took a customary trip to Louisville from his home at the Abbey of Gethsemani in the hills of rural Kentucky. Suddenly, standing at the corner of Fourth Street and Walnut, Brother Louis (whom we know better by his birth name, Thomas Merton) had a rapturous vision of the beauty and oneness of humanity:

> In Louisville, at the center of the shopping district, I was suddenly overwhelmed with the realization that I loved all those people, that they were mine and I theirs, that we could not be alien to one another even though we were total strangers. . . . It is a glorious destiny to be a member of the human race.

As Merton reflected more on this experience, he penned some of the loveliest lines in twentieth-century contemplative writing:

> There is no way of telling people that they are all walking around shining like the sun. . . . I suddenly saw the secret beauty of their hearts, the depths of their hearts where neither sin nor desire nor self-knowledge can reach, the core of their reality, the

person that each one is in God's eyes. If only they could all see themselves as they really are. If only we could see each other that way all of the time. There would be no more war, no more hatred, no more cruelty, no more greed.[1]

A few summers ago, on a humid afternoon in early August, I found myself standing at Brother Louis's grave on the grounds of Gethsemani. The marker is a simple cross and would certainly be passed over by a visitor looking for a tourist attraction. It seemed appropriate in light of the oneness Merton saw so clearly; while he surely shined like the sun, so did everyone.

I was at the abbey because my friend Dave, a wild-haired, charismatic poet, had invited me to hang out with him. I had become acquainted with his project he called "Antler" and wanted to learn more. He and I were introduced through mutual friends, and once we started chatting, he thought I might be interested in art and faith intersections, or "sacred collisions"—a favorite image of his. The trip would inspire us and give us clarity.

Like many autistic people, I do much better in the company of one or two friends I trust, rather than in larger gatherings. So the promise of a community of faith, almost like church small groups that would meet mostly in intimate settings, was especially appealing to me. And Dave himself was and is appealing to me for another very autistic reason: he's honest and authentic, some might say to a fault. The guy has Old Testament prophet energy. I'd hang out with him over your typical inane small-talker ninety-nine times out of a hundred.

* * *

What was Antler? And why did it matter to me and others, then and now?

We talked on the winding Kentucky back roads as we drove from Louisville to Gethsemani. I understood that Merton would function as a kind of patron saint for the project, and that his epiphany would be a touchstone in Antler's formation. Gethsemani, too, would play a part in the group's development.

I learned the big picture: Antler (which took its name from the William Stafford poem "A Message from the Wanderer") existed to promote creativity for spiritual growth, where faith and imagination could be cultivated by individuals and small groups. It was not a website or literary journal or small press or group that meets once a month or year—though it took some of those forms at different times. Antler embodied, as Makoto Fujimura has written about, the true meaning of shalom: not just the absence of terror or war but the integration of the self and community toward wholeness.[2] If there is "no way of telling people that they are all walking around shining like the sun," Antler mattered because it might at least point us in the right direction, give us glimpses of "[our]selves as [we] really are," at the core of our being.

. . .

Dave was well read in Merton's work and also had developed a friendship with Brother Paul Quenon, who had been at Gethsemani Abbey for over fifty years, spending the first part of his monastic life working directly with Merton. After Vespers, Brother Paul, Dave, and I sat on a hillside overlooking the monastery's extensive grounds, eating a dinner of cheese and bread made by the monks and sipping red wine that had warmed in the afternoon heat. Each of us recited a poem from memory at Brother Paul's behest. Then we talked about current events and told stories from our personal journeys. The sound of crickets was broken by the bell tolling for Compline. We realized we'd lost track of time, so we rushed Brother Paul back to the abbey for the service.

Later, I would recall the blend of bread and wine and storytelling with prayer and the observing of silence: the cadence of the afternoon would be a good model for the rhythm of Antler's work.

. . .

After Compline, we met Brother Paul again and headed far across the fields toward a lake. We would end the hot Kentucky day with a swim.

On the top of a hill, we discovered another pilgrim sitting on a bench praying. He'd come alone to retreat at the abbey for a long weekend.

"Join us!" we offered. He did.

Wildflowers I could not name dotted the rolling pastures on the way to the lake. The lake, too, was unnamed. Without ceremony, we undressed and stood nakcd together for a brief moment before plunging off a rock into the cool water. We swam out to the middle of the lake and began a conversation that would last until dark, when bats began circling overhead and swooping down. And in those moments, we belonged: we "could not be alien to one another" even though a few of us were total strangers. The depth, honesty, and inclusivity not often possible in larger faith gatherings could be nurtured here, even for an autistic. And the whole thing was a little over-the-top, marked by mystery, which appealed to the artist in me. This: this was Antler.

. . .

The vision of Antler would be realized slowly, haphazardly, but also vigorously. The idea grew organically, shunning formal status and instead acting as a kind of magnet, drawing together and shaping relationships among artists and other wayfarers.

As word got out, people continued to inquire. Many of them were like me: they seemed to be at home neither in the church nor in the world; they were simultaneously residents and aliens in both places. And their writing was often unsuited to the current corporate models: their stories were "too religious" to garner mainstream appeal, yet too radical, honest, or real to be picked up by religious publishers. Most of these writers, thank God, have been unwilling to sanitize their narratives to pass the censors. But that leaves them with few good options.

Antler listened to the heartbeat of this movement and began facilitating community through the telling of our stories. We gravitated toward work that respected reality and the diverse ways in which faith works to shape our identities for the good. We didn't want half-truths that ignored and repressed the shadow side, but rather stories and poems and essays that spoke to and modeled what the Antler community wanted to accomplish—work that let us see ourselves as we really are.

Alan W. Jones, dean emeritus of Grace Cathedral in San Francisco, has written, "What does reimagining religion involve? Exchanging the dogmatic stance of certainty for the way of imagination, which is not frightened by the thought that God is greater than religion."[3]

It seems to me that Antler had a part to play in reimagining religion—which, I think, is perhaps not as sweeping as it sounds. All it takes is people with a shared vision, something akin, perhaps, to Merton's vision of the beauty and oneness of humanity. Such a space attracted me as an autistic Christian. I needed small but inclusive groups that would spur authenticity and honesty; a flexible model in the face of the stodgy expectations of the conventional parish; but also a link to church history, tradition, and liturgy. Outings to the abbey—and the dozens of retreats and events that would follow in the coming years—became my life-giving ancillary to church, my small group.

Marilyn Nelson once said to a gathering of us artists, "Follow your vision. You must believe that there are people out there who are hungry for what only you can give them." And so the Antler journey began: built on imagination and shalom, shunning the need to be right. Like four ordinary men in an unnamed Kentucky lake, Antler was a place to be naked and vulnerable in order to be baptized, to give up the easy cynicisms of our age, and to emerge with a vision for who we are at the core of our reality. It has had an enormous impact on me to this day.

Merton wrote, "It is a glorious destiny to be a member of the human race." In the end, I think that's what I wanted to do through the deepening of the relationships afforded to me by Antler: celebrate our glorious destiny as members of the human race. And give thanks to the Creator who sustains us.

Antler has evolved past its initial expression. Over the years it changed me and many of my best friends. I'll quote Dave in an interview with *Ruminate* magazine around the time of the founding of Antler, to explain in his words what it was meant for:

Ruminate: So, then, where did you first see a real need for imagination and creativity in religious communities?

Dave: My perception in all this was and is something not so much seen acutely but perceived—invisible forces setting a compass needle spinning. But I'm also operating under the assumption that my needle is close to calibrated, and that's iffy. To preface: I don't have the answers, but am in a seeking posture, which means I'm working . . . though pragmatically that means I often turn out more questions than answers—tough break for me and others that might look to [Antler] for [clarity].

Enter the idea and experiment of Antler (and sacred collisions!) . . . aiming to help people interested in this intersection of faith and imagination find it, cultivate it, and allow it to change their lives and communities.[4]

It was always about asking better questions, adopting a posture of seeking and finding fellowship with others who noticed the sacred collisions. What we offered the man sitting on the hilltop at the abbey, I offer you now: Join us. Create your own inclusive small group of faithful misfits, a band of "both/and" people who will exchange fidelity to "either/or" dogmas for the imaginative love of God and neighbor. Or perhaps you already have such a group. Either way, pray with me: Lord of Hosts, the sun is still shining. Lead us to the water that we may plunge in. Amen.

SERVICE AND THE SPECTRUM

Each of you should use whatever gift you have received to serve others, as faithful stewards of God's grace in its various forms.

—1 Peter 4:10

What does it mean for a person to be a "faithful steward of God's grace"? How does it look specifically from the autism spectrum?

* * *

My church has a ministry, held two Sundays a month, nick-named the Lunch Box. It's a free, hot midday dinner served in the fellowship hall after coffee time has concluded and most of the congregation has left. The south doors open to folks who don't normally join us for service. They are lined up down the street and even around the corner.

Numbers range from sixty to over one hundred, depending on the week. Many attendees are homeless. Some are mentally ill. Some are veterans of military service with complex PTSD and other conditions. In the winter, they are often wearing rags that offer little protection from the cold.

All of them are hungry: the poverty rate in the Rust Belt city of Marion, Indiana, is a staggering 25.9 percent.[1] Yes, more than a quarter of the people live below the poverty line—much higher than the national average in the US, which is still very high at between 10 and 11 percent.[2]

In Matthew 25, Jesus describes the King separating the sheep and the goats. His words ring with range and resonance across the centuries: "For I was hungry and you gave me something to eat, I was thirsty and you gave me something to drink, I was a stranger and you invited me in" (v. 35).

And when the righteous person asked him, "When did we see you and do these things?" the King answered, "Truly I tell you, whatever you did for one of the least of these brothers and sisters of mine, you did for me" (v. 40).

The Lunch Box makes perfect sense in this context, and I'm so glad to attend a church that serves our community in this way.

Except I take no part in it.

. . .

Let me explain. Many neurotypical Christians don't need to claim deeply personal ownership over their service decisions—they can often be "plugged in" to a ministry, per church parlance. They can fill in at the Lunch Box without thinking a whole lot about what it will cost them emotionally, without rearranging their entire week. Or they can even do something a bit more time-consuming: serve a term on the vestry or teach a Sunday school lesson.

Those decisions, while reorienting people's time and energy, likely will not undo them. Those same decisions might well undo me.

Counting the Cost: The Autistic Reckoning

Autistic people have to forge a new path forward every single time, a unique path that takes into account the levels of all our equalizer sliders: mental, emotional, and physical energy (each depletes much more quickly and erratically than for neurotypicals); alone/recharging time; sensory inputs and comfort level (temperature, clothing options in a wide variety of situations, sounds, lighting, smells, singular or multiple sources of each type of sensory input, duration); time of day; whether or not we're being valued for our strengths and accommodated for our needs rather than excluded for perceived deficits; and much more.

I have to own this reckoning completely, and differently, every single time.

Because I have to engage life at such a profound level in order to enter into any Christian service, the good news is that it generally has a transformative effect on me . . . if I can say yes. I must stop and consider the lilies of the field, to locate and apprehend the greater beauty and purpose in an act of faith, to take stock of it and me, even to chronicle and frame and articulate it to myself and others, much more so than the average person does. They can roll with the changes. I have to count the cost, and because I do, I know what it's doing to me, how it's changing me, inviting me to transformation, to renaissance, to being born again over and over through each sacrament of service, each month, each year. My faith does not remain stagnant; by design, it can't.

The bad news is, I have to say no a lot. This is because I've counted the cost and it would, without question, leave me gravely in the red.

Let us say our priest asks for an additional Lunch Box volunteer one week. Many people can say, "Sure, I'll do it."

I'm autistic. I will be thinking:

How does it work? What is my specific role? Will our roles be clear? Who is in charge? What expectations will they have that they will never specify out loud but will assume everyone understands? (Classic neurotypical behavior.) Will they get frustrated with me for asking a lot of questions and waiting for clear direction rather than just "getting it" and taking initiative? (In my experience, people nearly always do.)

I'll replay in my head every service opportunity I accepted that went poorly the first time around, and how embarrassed and depleted it left me and how I never wanted to leave my couch again. Then I'll return to the list of questions. Because I need to know. I need to know it all.

How long will it take? Am I cleaning up afterward too? What if more people come than they expect—will there be enough food? Will I have to rearrange my whole afternoon, and will it screw up my routine and cause a meltdown tonight? When was my last meltdown? Is my family still upset about it? How will this affect the atmosphere of my home for the coming week? Month?

Will people talk to me? Am I expected to talk with them—about what? Jesus and the Good News? The weather? Is there some sort of official programming? Will someone pray or preach? Will someone ask me to pray? Many are homeless or in poor mental health—how will this impact the nature of our conversation? Will I be able to handle the smell of body odor combined with the other strong scents in the room?

What food is being made? If the entire kitchen smells like eggs, I will get sick and have to leave—I have a sensory issue with the smell and texture and color of eggs, especially scrambled. But if I say this to anyone, they'll think I'm super weird or trying to get out of doing the work. I will likely be more trouble than I'm worth.

And there it is: *Is there a net good being accomplished here? And if so, at what cost to my health?* It always comes back to counting the cost.

· · ·

In Luke 14:28–30, Jesus talks about counting the cost of discipleship. He says, "Suppose one of you wants to build a tower. Won't you first sit down and estimate the cost to see if you have enough money to complete it? For if you lay the foundation and are not able to finish it, everyone who sees it will ridicule you, saying, 'This person began to build and wasn't able to finish.'"

I have to count the cost of following Jesus into that fellowship hall to set tables or into that kitchen to prepare food. Only it's usually not financial cost that I'm estimating. It's a different kind of capital.

It's my well-being. It's my very life.

So sometimes, without anyone knowing the cost-counting that went into my decision, I will have to say no. Then I'll worry that I have a different problem, a Matthew 7:19 problem.

Bearing Fruit

Matthew 7:19–20 tells us, "Every tree that does not bear good fruit is cut down and thrown into the fire. Thus, by their fruit you will recognize them."

Can I say no to service and ministry as often as my autistic needs dictate and still bear good fruit? If so, what will that need to look like? Will it lead to feelings of worthlessness and shame because there's a perception that I'm not doing my part? The truth is that, yes, it often does. But I'm also called to be a "faithful steward of God's grace" in other areas, and perhaps those too are fruit-bearing trees in Christ's orchard.

The fruit I bear in my home, as a husband and father, will be better if I say no to public opportunities I know will compromise my mental and physical health. For years, especially prediagnosis, I had a tendency to do what the world asked me to, in the precise ways it asked me to do it, in order to advance my career as an academic or writer, or to please someone in church, usually the minister. For years I prepared and led worship in a band, attending practices midweek and early in the morning before service, and feeling a weight of responsibility for the encounter parishioners experienced. I always believed that the greater good was that, by saying yes to so many requests, I would be serving my family in the long run by carving out a place of good standing in the community—that any short-term discomfort would be worth it.

But I lacked balance and perspective. You can only push yourself over the limit so many times, can only melt down so often upon entering the door to your house, before you ruin everything you love. You can only cocoon yourself in your blanket to stare at endless food shows featuring a droll host eating strange carnival concoctions at county fairs, his vapid banter as fluffy as the cotton candy in his hand, before the very foundations of your life begin to crumble. And aggressive capitalism—and churches that operate within its parameters—will always reward your hard work with pressure to work even harder. Soon you find yourself spiraling out of control.

So I say no. And yet. I can worship God, pray, and love my neighbor in small everyday ways here and there, but I still need to negotiate James's idea that faith without works is dead. How do we define "works"? For me, these days I'll often pass on an opportunity for public service in favor of planned time with Beth and the kids. First Timothy 5:8 would seem to favor this balance: "Anyone who does not provide for their relatives, and especially for their own household, has denied the faith and is worse than an unbeliever."

Likewise, the power I hold in my sphere of influence on campus—the classroom—is perhaps in some ways more immediate and sustained than that of outside volunteer service, so I focus on that role. I pray for my students; I pray *with* them. I put in many hours reading novels, poems, and memoirs by diverse writers so I'll attain knowledge and wisdom, a sharper sense of how we exert control over language, and a richer feel for the varieties of being alive around the world. I attend conferences and workshops on pedagogy and lead trips to London and Edinburgh. I have coffee with students; I listen and guide them as they work out their own salvation with requisite fear and trembling. Grading can be done in a coffee shop, alone, with music playing in my noise-canceling headphones. I control my time and energy, then bring that balance to bear on the love I can show the students in person as I teach and mentor.

Also, the poignancy of producing the written word—an act I can complete in solitude according to the demands of my inner calendar, an act that God has prepared me for since childhood, a domain in which God has given me gifts to steward . . . here I can make a difference and, if God wills it, I may have an audience. I can recognize that my calling will necessitate a lot of the work being done behind the scenes, out of the public eye. I can wrestle with big-picture concepts, vivid and specific descriptive details, lyrical elegance, syntactic economy, and everything else I need to honor the call to write well. I can write and read more in order to grow into an artist of greater impact.

I've had to widen my faith to include a belief that these acts of faithful service are no less worship than serving a hot meal to the homeless. They are simply better suited for me as an autistic with very specific boundaries and limitations . . . and gifts.

· · ·

This reckoning does have practical implications. When I'm up for promotion, for example, there is a section on community service, and I need to have some things listed on that section. How do I show the powers that be that I am a part of the body of no less value than the ones they recognize more easily? I turn to 1 Corinthians 12.

One Body, Many Parts: 1 Corinthians 12:12–26

Unity and Diversity in One Body

Just as a body, though one, has many parts, but all its many parts form one body, so it is with Christ. For we were all baptized by one Spirit so as to form one body—whether Jews or Gentiles, slave or free—and we were all given the one Spirit to drink. Even so the body is not made up of one part but of many.

Now if the foot should say, "Because I am not a hand, I do not belong to the body," it would not for that reason stop being part of the body. And if the ear should say, "Because I am not an eye, I do not belong to the body," it would not for that reason stop being part of the body. If the whole body were an eye, where would the sense of hearing be? If the whole body were an ear, where would the sense of smell be? But in fact God has placed the parts in the body, every one of them, just as he wanted them to be. If they were all one part, where would the body be? As it is, there are many parts, but one body.

The eye cannot say to the hand, "I don't need you!" And the head cannot say to the feet, "I don't need you!" On the contrary, those parts of the body that seem to be weaker are indispensable, and the parts that we think are less honorable we treat with special honor. And the parts that are unpresentable are treated with special modesty, while our presentable parts need no special treatment. But God has put the body together, giving greater honor to the parts that lacked it, so that there should be no division in the body, but that its parts should have equal concern for each other. If one part suffers, every part suffers with it; if one part is honored, every part rejoices with it. (1 Corinthians 12:12–26)

What if we substitute "neurotypicals and autistics" for "Jews or Gentiles"? Or what if we substitute for "a message of wisdom" given through the Spirit (v. 8), "miraculous powers" (v. 10), and so forth for that which is carried out in my church (Lunch Box, altar guild, vestry, nursery, etc.) and in my life (writing, teaching, marriage, parenting, etc.)?

Then might we conclude, through the insight of the Scriptures and the gift of a twenty-first-century understanding of neurobiology, something like this:

"Dan is autistic and has told us he'd rather be with little Ethan in the nursery than doing the serving at the Lunch Box. Rocking a baby soothes both him and the baby, whereas the social interaction at the Lunch Box can get hectic and unpredictable depending on who shows up any given week. John is well-suited for Lunch Box—he's a talker, and strangers are drawn to him. Susan is a talented cook and would be great for making the pot roast. She's a wheelchair user, and the church has not had the budget to update the kitchen to make it ADA compliant. So how about Lee, who wants to start logging volunteer hours for his college applications, work with Susan in the kitchen, handing her items from the high shelves and cabinets? That would be a great entry point into Lunch Box: learning where everything goes."

Maybe this is an impractical fantasy, a naïve and corny pipe dream. Or could it be "the work of one and the same Spirit, and he distributes them to each one, just as he determines" (v. 11)? Could this be an inclusive strategy for the faithful church—a way to make faith, with works, accessible and alive for all who desire to serve? Indeed, could it be, "Thy kingdom come . . . on earth as it is in heaven"?

I want to think so. But it would take a depth of comprehension and accommodation that the church often lacks. By accommodation, I don't mean "special treatment"—I mean that each person be known and encouraged to serve in accordance with their gifts. We would need to invest in our communities in order to know each other intimately; only then could we feel safe communicating openly, telling our stories, being heard. We would need to know without a doubt that we are affirmed and accepted by the body in both our strengths and limitations.

We would have to trust our autistic and neurodivergent members, knowing that they've counted the cost and made a balanced decision: balanced not in favor of personal comfort but of being appropriately challenged in an area of service, rather than needlessly mismatched, overwhelmed, and putting one's self at risk of harm.

Perhaps this is something like what the apostle Paul means at the end of 1 Corinthians 12, when he writes, "I will show you the most excellent way."

DANCING IN FIELDS OF WHEAT AND TARES

Chicago is cold and gray. I'm stuck at O'Hare for my connecting flight to Buffalo en route home. At 4:00 a.m. mountain time, I caught a shuttle bus from Santa Fe to the airport in Albuquerque, having just completed a ten-day residency as part of my MFA program in creative writing at Seattle Pacific University. Our summer residency takes place at St. John's College in the high desert alongside the Glen Workshop, a program of art and faith that attracts poets, musicians, novelists, visual artists, and others from around the country.

The company of like-minded folks was intoxicating. Here at the airport, I reckon with the fact that the earth is not peopled primarily with artists like the ones I met at the Glen. It is peopled with people. So I watch them.

A twentysomething couple holding hands negotiates the terminal at a brisk clip, wheeling efficient luggage behind them. A moment later, an elderly woman with a cane almost gets hit by an airport golf cart beeping its horn. The driver seems determined to stay cheerful though frustration is evident beneath her smile. But the old woman is oblivious to the sound of the horn and, more frightening, to the general flow and pace of this world.

Then, a singularly odd image: a guy who could not be more than thirty sports one eyebrow almost entirely silver. A double take, and what I hope is a stealthy triple take, confirms. His left eyebrow is the color of his hair—dark brown. His right is at least three-quarters the color of the hair of a man twice his age, an airy but slick silver, unmistakable as the Crayola I reached for to color stars in the skies of my childhood.

The idiosyncrasy unsettles me. I want to go online and burn time, but I had put my laptop in my checked bag. I decide to go for a walk. At the gift shop, ten thousand charms gleam from shelves—Windy City T-shirts, hoodies, ball caps in a range of colors and styles. Point-of-purchase impulse items display in descending order of novelty. On top, at eye level, is a new one to me: piña colada bubble gum. I settle on Tic-Tacs.

But I cannot forget the silver eyebrow, wayward twin of Normal. I return to my departing gate and the young man remains where I left him. I cannot shake his innocuous but jarring irregularity, as though his face holds the paradox of innocence and experience together in tension. He seems to somehow stand figuratively between the woman with the cane for whom the airport is a veritable gauntlet and the young couple who could circumnavigate it all day and get up tomorrow to do it again. He seems to wear on the outside what we get to hide from or put off: our own slow march toward greater imperfection, and then the end.

. . .

Richard Rohr has defined suffering as "whenever you are not in control."[1] Control equals power, the gratification of the ego. Last night represented the fulfillment of a dream: to meet Father Rohr in person. I'd only known him through his books, meditations on weighty topics like suffering, contemplative prayer, centering, and respect for mystery. His talk last night touched on non-dual thinking and the notion that reality, seen through the awareness that comes with the inner authority gained from suffering, is less clear than we like to believe.

He spoke of Jesus's mandate to let the wheat and the tares grow together and let God have control in the end—God who is not threatened by the presence of tares. If we took it upon ourselves to start weeding the field, we would get it wrong. We would proceed by making false distinctions, in groups and out groups, positions of advantage and positions of humiliation. We would grab power and disenfranchise anyone who didn't fit the narrative we created; we would pluck out wheat and call it tares.

. . .

We know that this mess is not hypothetical. Ignoring the message to let it all grow together, we do what Jesus told us to avoid doing. We take his parables and drain them of mystery in order to construct theological systems. We seem to think that if we extrapolate correctly, we can develop a rule book for how to live. This accounts for too much of religion's work in the world. However necessary these systems are, there is often no room for paradox or mystery. We feel free to exclude anyone who doesn't fit. We know it's not faith—it's merely control, the fleeting and futile avoidance of suffering. It's the opposite of the way of Jesus, a way that privileges the powerless, the weak, the suffering, and others from whom we often just look away.

Filmmaker Akira Kurosawa said, "The role of an artist is to not look away."[2] The service Father Rohr presided over was an anointing service for artists of Christian faith. We sang and read responsively, he spoke, and then he and three others took bowls of oil with which to anoint us—to, as Father Rohr said, "give us a permission we had probably never received from the church," the anointing to make art that respects the suffering that leads to seeing.

We were anointed for the creation of art that does not look away but looks more deeply and maybe finds the courage to celebrate what is called tares, including those who, under control-based social and religious systems, have been rooted out. Historically, this has included neurodivergent people who were institutionalized, frequently from early childhood through death. The privilege of anointing meant that I could use my own voice to tell tare stories, that I would not be rooted out or spoken over anymore.

We were anointed to see that it is often in these dismissed ones, even "the least of these," where we find beauty. Unlike the temporal beauty of the young-and-in-control traipsing through the airport, this beauty haunts, instructs, and endures.

I stood in line to receive the anointing from Father Rohr. As I came face-to-face with this spiritual giant, I saw that he was, like me, a small man. His unassuming Franciscan spirit became palpable; his touch was imperfect and tender as a new parent's. His oiled thumb crossed my forehead as he blessed me in a near whisper. Then he placed his palm on the top of my head and held it there longer than I expected, as if this ritual were more than mere ceremony but an important physical act unto itself.

. . .

Aware of the thick substance on my forehead, I reminded myself many times that night not to accidentally rub it off. I wanted the oil of my anointing to stay, to reorient me, to remind me that the rain falls on the just and the unjust, that in this both/ and world, I must refuse what tempts me daily: the arrogance to think that my particular group and I have discovered the final distinguishing features of tares and are just now heading out the door to do some weeding.

I want to be an artist who does not look away, who honors the messy real. I wanted the oil cross to be like a silver eyebrow, a boon, a reminder that real beauty is not even a simple turning of the tables that makes the first last and the last first—it is instead a revelation, a vision fierce enough to hold us all and to reconcile that which cannot be reconciled, like a lion and a lamb.

After the service I met Father Rohr, had a beer with him, fumbled to articulate what his work has meant to me. I think I managed to say something like "there is no way I'd be a person of faith right now" without his writings. He seemed happy to hear it but didn't give me any sage advice. We made small talk about our hometowns (he's from Kansas).

I asked a friend to take a picture of us. In it, I'm red-faced, sweating in the warm room and in my nervousness. I had over-eaten at the St. John's cafeteria all week and felt bloated. Father Rohr is not exactly Hollywood leading man material either. His eyes are partially obscured by thick glasses, and his bald skull reflects the light. It's a bad picture, but the photographer did not look away. It's real, so perhaps it's good.

· · ·

The night wore on. Father Rohr and most others had long since gone to bed, leaving just us MFA students. We were tired too, but our residency was decidedly not over, not yet. One last time we entered the great hall, a kind of Heorot where all week famous artists, our heroes, had held banquets of truth, beauty, and goodness. Now the chairs were pushed aside. Someone hooked a laptop to the PA system and pumped dance tracks. Heorot became a discotheque.

Some danced right away, at home in the kinesthetic world of rhythm and movement. Some even danced well. But for the most part, I suppose we are people destined to make art with pens and keyboards, not arms and legs. I, for one, am terribly self-conscious; I do not dance well and am never in a hurry to demonstrate it. But we needed to celebrate ten intensive days of art and faith before heading home to our own communities around the country, places where we might not have permission—where, like salmon in a Central New York October, we may well tire from swimming upstream.

A classmate invited me out to the floor, to the circle that had formed. I made a face that I thought sufficiently indicated my reluctance. But her face carried a message too: one of pure joy. A middle-aged woman who has both suffered and celebrated her share in this world, she took my hand as tenderly as Father Rohr had touched my head. She looked at me and did not look away.

What choice did I have? I went. I tried to dance. Awkward and unsure and very, very autistic, I looked around horrified. Then I looked at the other equally imperfect souls in the circle. Then I closed my eyes and listened. I stopped trying to dance, to be in control, and just did it, just danced. Just celebrated everything, wheat and tares. I danced for a long time. Then I reached up to wipe the sweat from my forehead, surprised by a handful of oil.

WRITING, TEACHING, AND LEARNING

If we pursue our stories, honestly and truly, they will send us on a pilgrimage that takes us, like Abraham, from one land to another, from a land of unknowing and darkness, through, of course, wastelands, where the promise of a promised land appears invisible and impossible . . . but the writing inexorably, day by day, moves us closer to clarity, to wisdom, to the very city of God, if we allow it.

—Leslie Leyland Fields, "Does the World
Really Need Your Story?"

AUTISM AND POETRY

Like most writers, I was drawn to language early. Mrs. Noonan, our librarian at Harry M. Fisher Elementary School in Mohawk, New York, read us *The Lion, the Witch and the Wardrobe* and *A Wrinkle in Time*, creating a storehouse of images and sounds that brought me distinct pleasure. In third grade, I read the Three Investigators series, discovering what John Gardner called "the vivid and continuous dream" of story.[1] Although books helped me escape a world I didn't fit into, I could feel that there was more to them than that; I sensed even then that good writing somehow increased me.

I couldn't articulate any of this, but as a kid I was becoming aware that books offered order and meaning while wrestling with the deepest ambiguities of the self and the world. Books brought me hope and put me in touch with idiosyncratic reality like nothing else did. I could always navigate a story, for there was a beginning, a middle, and an end. In books, I was never awkward and, even better, I was never unwelcome.

I was a poor student in high school. The challenges of undiagnosed autism made it hard: terrible struggles with executive functioning (time management, starting and finishing tasks, prioritizing and organizing work) and a host of sensory challenges always plagued me.

Yet poetry was in my soul, if buried. English was my strong suit, and I excelled in it when I—as all my teachers exhorted me to do—"applied myself." In my senior year of high school, I read two books that gave me direction for my future: J. D. Salinger's *The Catcher in the Rye* and W. P. Kinsella's *Shoeless Joe*. Works like these offered the beginnings of answers to perennial coming-of-age questions: Who am I? Who do I want to be? What should I do? Thoreau said, "The mass of men lead lives of quiet desperation," and that rang true in the town where I grew up. I wanted to avoid such a fate. I would end up going to college. I would study English. And I would come to poetry.

. . .

As I began my first serious attempts at writing, poetry seemed a natural choice. I liked the precision and acuteness of the language. And I felt overwhelmed with the sustained richness of novels I read in my college classes and on my own, magnificent books like *Jane Eyre* and *One Hundred Years of Solitude* and *Fathers and Sons*. The long form intimidated me; I felt that if I would ever successfully leverage my pitiful reserve of talent in the service of creation, it would need to be on a much smaller scale . . . like a poem.

Along with economy of form came the knowledge that poetry has been considered the highest art of language, "the best words in their best order," as Coleridge put it. I liked that poetry gave me achievable goals, and the case could be made that through poetry I worked at the pinnacle of what language could do. Most importantly, though, I simply fell in love with poems I read. (Only decades later would I discover that imagery in poetry—elements that engage the five senses—were particularly appealing to me because, like most autistics, I think in pictures. Poetry was a natural fit for my neurodivergent brain wiring.)

I began reading poetry in earnest, obsessing over tiny masterpieces I discovered. My spare minutes and dollars earned washing dishes at the college dining hall vanished at Brown Bag Bookshop and Rick's Recycled Books and the Goodwill, Salvation Army, and Volunteers of America stores in Rochester. I picked up beautiful volumes published by the press in town, BOA Editions—collections by William Heyen, Dorianne Laux, Li-Young Lee, Lucille Clifton, Naomi Shihab Nye. I grabbed books by famous names and names I'd never seen before and haven't since. I took anthologies out of the library, copying by hand into a journal lines and entire poems that spoke to me. I fell hard for the soaring verse of Federico García Lorca; I carried around a beat-up paperback of Robert Bly's *Silence in the Snowy Fields*. I studied journals like *Virginia Quarterly Review*, *The Bitter Oleander*, and *Mudfish*, along with those regal benchmarks *Poetry*, the *New Yorker*, and the *Atlantic Monthly*.

I filled up pages simply because it thrilled me.

I published my first poem at age twenty-one in an issue of a journal that contained work by James Tate, who had just won the Pulitzer Prize. The satisfaction of that moment—not just seeing my name and work in print but also joining "the Great Conversation"—proved too strong to resist, and I began sending out to magazines around the country. Most came back with form rejections.

I learned. I failed better. I remembered why I loved reading and writing in the first place; I tried, in one of my favorite phrases of '90s pop culture, to "keep it real"; and I went from there.

. . .

I still try to go from there. Whether I'm taking my own kids to the library or developing new poems, I try not to get cynical, overwhelmed, or seduced by fads. The wonders of literature remain true, even when my life gets messy and my mind gets ugly and I see the people around me as something other than a little lower than the angels. Like Galway Kinnell's sow being blessed by Saint Francis, I need to relearn beauty, and often. Poetry retains its unique ability to do just that: to instruct at the most profound levels of being.

Like the boy sitting on the floor of Harry M. Fisher Elementary School library, I still delight in sensory imagery and sound. I know that the discipline of writing poetry enables meaning and hope rather than desperation, and I know that language used well increases us all.

THE INSIDIOUS NATURE OF BAD CHRISTIAN STORIES

When I was a child, I talked like a child, I thought like a child, I reasoned like a child. When I became a man, I put the ways of childhood behind me.

—1 Corinthians 13:11

In the wake of another awful movie version of a popular "Christian" novel, one of the worst recent attempts at shoehorning conservative theology into story, I am mostly smiling at the hilariously bad reviews (it sits at a mind-boggling 1 percent on Rotten Tomatoes) and spending my time and money on good art, which always abounds.

Yet, because I'm a person of faith and an artist, I fear that someone might associate me with such kitsch. It's important to me to both distance myself from it and articulate why: not because it's merely tacky or lowbrow but because it's far more insidious.

Bad storytelling is bad theology, forwarding an immature view of God, self, and neighbor. And in my case as a creative writing professor, failing to call out bad storytelling is also bad teaching.

Now, many Christian readers of serious books and viewers of good films have probably worked out these issues some time ago with the help of great writers and thinkers. Even a majority of my Christian college students—some only a year or two removed from an upbringing loaded with propaganda—have grown out of it, and for that I am eternally grateful.

But some have not, and they are only now encountering serious challenges to the paradigms held up by the insular communities in which they were raised. Also—sadly—a small division inside my own learning community encourages formulaic "Christian" writing, and holds up as a model the kind of campy rubbish I mentioned at the outset of this essay.

So, while many have done it before and much better, I will briefly add my voice to those who have distinguished between good storytelling and bad in the context of Christian faith. Autistics circle back to honesty over and over as a touchstone of authentic identity and relationship. Bad storytelling is dishonest and therefore repulses me as both an autistic person and a Christ follower.

Since I feel that most examples of bad Christian art don't deserve serious critical attention, I've decided to talk in the abstract here, aware of the dangers of that choice. I do think that if you fill in the example of your liking, much of the critique will work much of the time; in my experience, most bad Christian stories are bad in similar ways.

For now, I want to focus on the fact that bad Christian stories are prescriptive. Though they may contain characters and a plot, they exist not to discover or examine truth but to deliver a message. In that way they're similar to propaganda used by oppressive regimes in times of war and genocide in attempts to control and manipulate people.

As such, bad Christian art is ironically neither Christian nor art. It cannot reflect a multifaceted, mysterious, and paradoxical God or God's creation. As Ron Hansen has put it:

So-called Christian fiction is often in fact pallid allegory, or a form of sermonizing, or is a reduction into formula . . . sometimes yielding to a Manichean dualism wherein good and evil are plainly at war. . . . We cannot call a fiction Christian just because there is no irreligion in it, no skepticism, nothing to cause offense, for such a fiction, in its evasions, may have evaded, in Karl Rahner's words, "that blessed peril that consists in encountering God."[1]

Good stories, on the other hand, are complex, containing layers and shades of meaning that aren't easily exhausted, even by attentive multiple readings. The best stories, as John Gardner argues, have an inherent moral dimension; immersive engagement with them helps us grow.[2] In their fidelity to the true and diverse nature of things (especially people), good stories tend to oppose "either/or" dichotomies. They develop empathy and compassion in readers by allowing us to imaginatively inhabit the lives of characters who are different from us in essential ways.

In short, good storytelling is honest.

Bad stories are calculated and disingenuous, the opposite of the childlike state of wonder that Jesus held up as a faith ideal and writers like C. S. Lewis helped to flesh out for generations of readers. Instead, bad Christian stories are child*ish*, playing to immature expressions of faith.

Childish Ways

What are some childish attitudes that bad Christian stories feed into and encourage?

- The immature need to have correct beliefs, as opposed to the adult need to consider and examine diverse voices to develop critical thinking, empathy, and love.

(Anne Lamott reminds us that "the opposite of faith is not doubt, but certainty. Certainty is missing the point entirely. Faith includes noticing the mess, the emptiness and discomfort, and letting it be there until some light returns."[3])

- The immature need to be continually comforted, rather than the adult need to be comforted when afflicted, but also afflicted and challenged by difficult art when one has become too comfortable, even complacent, in one's faith, relationships, work, and leisure.

- The immature need for clear answers to questions that have none, as opposed to the adult need to learn to live creatively with mystery and paradox. What Keats called "negative capability" is helpful here: he described it as an "ability to contemplate the world without the desire to try and reconcile contradictory aspects or fit it into closed and rational systems."[4]

- The immature need to separate good and evil into clear camps at all times, as opposed to the adult need to learn to let the wheat and the tares grow together until the harvest.

- The immature confusing of real emotion and true empathy with shallow sentimentality and greeting card cliché, as opposed to the adult need to feel deeply through encounter and catharsis while confronting our own contradictions.

- The immature need to romanticize the past, interpreting, for example, the 1950s in America as a kind of moral golden age from which we're constantly slipping further away, as opposed to the adult need to recognize the complications, flaws, and entrenched injustices of every era—and in that recognition, to nevertheless work in faith to love God and our neighbors.

I suspect that many of these attitudes are the result of the immature need to be in control—as opposed to the adult need to learn to live in liminal spaces, to trust in and wait on God through ambiguity, to accept with serenity that which we cannot change, to pray for the courage to change what we can and should, and to humbly seek the wisdom to know the difference.

Teaching and Learning

The mission of the university where I teach is "to develop servant leaders marked with a passion to minister Christ's redemptive love and truth to a world in need."[5] The verb in that sentence—the thing for which I am responsible, the thing I'm supposed to be doing every day—is *develop*: to help people grow and progress; to bring them into fuller capability; to take them to a more advanced and effective state.

The word has an Old French origin: "dis" reverses or has a negative effect, and "voloper" means "to wrap" or "to envelop." So I'm supposed to unwrap: unwrap potential, foster student development by giving them every opportunity—through the two-steps-forward-one-step-back movement that accompanies hard work—to grow.

Wherever we encourage the consumption and production of dishonest stories, we fail to develop students. We fail to challenge them toward the growth we promise in our mission statement. Where we hold up bad art as a model, we become something less than a university, and we fall short of Paul's mark in his letter to the Corinthians: to put away immature attitudes.

Moreover, we fail to unwrap students' potential to minister—to love their neighbors as themselves—because bad Christian stories encourage them to see both themselves and their neighbors as being either right or wrong, good guys or bad guys. This particular failure is foundational.

. . .

So where does this leave us? Back to the power of good art.

Here's Richard Rohr: "The best criticism of the bad is the practice of the better."[6] I thank God daily that there is no shortage of great artists working in the realms of literature, film, painting, music, and everywhere else we glimpse our humanity and grow toward mature Christian faith. In fact, there is more great and deeply honest art than I or my students will ever have the time to contemplate over the course of our lifetimes. What wonderful news.

In the end, simply criticizing (and subsequently ignoring) dishonest stories won't do. Having considered the arguments against bad art, we must use our time encountering the best art, the most excellent and authentic stories available, works that, in form and content, challenge and provoke and console and develop us. Enuma Okoro sums up the power of good art in the context of Christian faith very well, and so she'll have the last word here:

> Good art points beyond itself and helps us recognize the human condition and the divine intrusion while calling us to more faithful relationship with the world, relationship that witnesses to the hope and redemption found in the Triune God and offered to us through Christ, the incarnate image that redeems all images grasping for God. . . . Artistic expression is a striving for more, a visual hunger for transcendental realities that can only be shaped out of what has already been given to us, unlike God who creates out of nothing. But like our Creator, such creative shaping can also lead to new realities we can live into.[7]

Amen.

BEAUTIFUL LOSER

Poetry at the Mall

Pray for one good humiliation every day.
　　　　—Richard Rohr, *Falling Upward*

I sit by the podium as an arts administrator I just met gives me
a long introduction. She must've pulled it from my website;
it's a full bio. Like, *really* full. She works through the names
of magazines where my poems have "appeared," and I wonder
what that word conveys to the uninitiated. Some of the journals
are obscure, what poets call "little magazines," while others are
better known. But in this space, all the titles are preposterous.

　　I was invited to read at the Artsgarden in Indianapolis. What
I don't know until I get there is that, on weekdays, the Artsgarden is glorified overflow seating for the mall food court.
This requires a quick adjustment of my expectations, a notion
utterly unrecognizable to my autistic brain.

　　Looking at the crowd, I get the sense that anyone listening
waits for a triumphant finish to my publication record, such as
the *New Yorker* or *Time*. When the index is done, though, their
expressions are pitiful. I've disappointed them, and I haven't
even begun to read yet.

The host tells folks that I was, in fact, born in Delaware but raised in New York. My discomfort increases. I try to ignore it. I fantasize that someone experiences the shock of recognition: "Ah . . . now I see the significance of the ocean imagery in his early work!"

Approaching the podium induces a bead of sweat to trickle from the pit of my arm down my right side. I think of a line from Thomas Hardy's poetry: "Down their carved names the rain-drop ploughs."[1] I feel absurd likening iconic post-Victorian calamity to sweating in the food court at lunch hour in Middle America. Yet even that leap seems reasonable compared to reading poetry at the mall.

I smile my crooked autistic smile and hold up my book, as if showing them something material will render me innocent of wrongdoing. I attempt a word on the relationship between poetry and place, a link that deeply informs my writing, but here the subject takes on a palpable irony. Out of options, I proceed toward the unthinkable: I read poems.

. . .

Since the space connects skywalks from corporate buildings to the mall proper, many people are passing through without stopping. A trio of businesswomen trails by, right in front of the podium, heels clacking loudly beneath pantsuits. They pay me no mind. The people at the tables are trapped, waiting for an opportune moment to slip out. Some appear visibly annoyed; others look curious, maybe even grateful. Most seem mildly embarrassed for me.

Poetry is a beautiful loser here. There's the sense it's a nice gesture, but the awkwardness overwhelms whatever glimpses of truth it might make available.

I get warmed up to the crowd insofar as that's possible. Then at some point in the reading, something clicks and I find myself at the other extreme, embracing the strangeness, ready to have some fun. Might as well, since, as I read poems, I discover that (a) I truly have no user-friendly poems anyway, and (b) I write about death much more than I realize.

To hell with it then: I get right up in the microphone to boom and echo my verse as far as my tenor will allow. I read the most surreal dreamscapes I've ever written; I emphasize the weirdest phrases. I read a poem where a man eating at a burger joint on the shore sees four of himself (one of whom is dead). The poem contains the lines, "I sold my feet at a trading post / in Lexington, Kentucky."

I look up innocently. There's a table of Indian men in polo shirts and Dockers, their hair and mustaches all neatly trimmed. They have stopped eating and are staring at me with equal parts confusion and contempt. I look back down at my book and read until my time is up.

Four people clap: the arts administrator, another poet, and two people sitting in the front who, I later learn, actually came for the reading.

· · ·

Okay, being on the spectrum surely can account for some of what I experienced that afternoon. But what a strange exercise: bringing poetry to an unsuspecting public. Poetry goes deep. The subject of death might come up, even more than once. As I learned in an Indianapolis mall, death probably shouldn't be considered at length in the food court on a Monday afternoon.

In a talk on why poetry matters, Mark Doty said, "Poetry . . . marks the place where one human being stood, bound in time, reporting what it is to be one. In the age of the collective of mass culture and mass market, there's hope in that."[2] Insofar as the American shopping mall represents mass culture, maybe it could use some poetry after all.

Maybe hope and humiliation are related. I've long claimed to want to make art that, as journalist Finley Peter Dunne said of newspapers, can "comfort the afflicted and afflict the comfortable." Only I never imagined *I* was the one who needed to get uncomfortable. I assumed I was fine. And I am—as long as I'm in my classroom, where nothing I say will be questioned in any elemental way. A student may disagree with me, but no one asks, "What's the deal with poetry?" or even, "Why are you doing this?"

And why not ask? It's an important question I don't often consider anymore from inside academia or the book world or whatever you call the place where I (mostly) live. It's a question that may cross the minds of people at the mall.

It's a question I need to confront anew if I want to avoid gaining the whole world but losing my own soul. That's the wrong kind of loss.

Richard Rohr says, "I tell holy people to pray for one good humiliation every day. I tell them to keep careful watch over their reaction to those humiliations. That is the way to avoid religious grandiosity and know that you are seeking God and not yourself."[3]

The loss of ego: that's the right kind of loss, the beautiful kind, filled with hope.

MEANING AND ESTRANGEMENT

Fiction is one long, sensuous derangement of familiarity through altered point of view. How would you recognize your world if it wasn't yours? What might you look and feel like if you weren't you? . . . Fiction plays on that overlap between self-composure and total, alien bewilderment, and it navigates by estrangement. . . . [The] act of bottomless, estranging kinship is probably the main goal of reading and writing novels. . . . Only inhabiting another's story can deliver us from certainty.

—Richard Powers, from a 2007 interview with *The Believer*

Creativity is a spiritual issue. Any progress is made by leaps of faith, some small and some large.

—Julia Cameron, *The Artist's Way*

It is the end of February and we just wrapped up the biennial Making Literature Conference at Taylor University: three exciting, challenging, and busy days of papers and essays, stories and poems, coffee and conversation. I worked fourteen-hour days and received so many texts and calls about flights and meals and room reservations that, were the small lake on campus not frozen solid, I entertained the idea of throwing my phone into it.

Now I'm hydrating, sleeping at night, reestablishing my precious routines and rituals, and seeing my family for periods of more than five minutes. And I'm ruminating on all the great things that happened. The conference was a lot of work, but it also brought a renewed sense of meaning.

Meaning abounded at Making Literature. African American poet Angela Shannon read a powerful work about the link between Jesus and B. B. King, about the Boston Marathon bombing of 2013, about water and memory and prayer. Miho Nonaka, a poet and scholar at Wheaton College, gave a brilliant paper on Shūsaku Endō's novel *Silence*, highlighting several passages in William Johnston's 1969 translation in light of intricacies in Japanese culture and language, and using Flannery O'Connor's ideas in *Mystery and Manners* as a critical lens. West Virginia novelist Jessie van Eerden spoke about "Midrashic impulse," and read from a gorgeous new work of fiction in which she renders scenes from the life of Rizpah, the woman in the Old Testament who was most famous for keeping a five-month vigil over the murdered bodies of the seven sons of Saul.

Making Literature is an undergraduate conference, so—though we treasure our keynotes—the students are the real stars, and their work makes up the bulk of the sessions. Student work was extraordinarily good. I heard visiting professors say things like, "That sounded more like an MFA reading than an undergraduate one," and "That paper might've been written by a colleague."

I was especially thrilled when we received the results for best creative work: the judge selected the graphic narrative "Dies Cinerum" by Bec Hartman, one of my own (best) students. The citation accompanying the award heaped praise on the piece; I hoped this would buoy the fatigued young artist. The word "painstaking" barely begins to suggest the number of hours

Bec spent not only crafting a sophisticated convergence of the story's dual narrative arcs but also completing thirty meticulous watercolor paintings, producing an acutely layered work.

Meaning. It enveloped us, reminded us that the solitary days and nights of devoted study and writing matter. As much as it was about awards, the gathering of community was itself a celebration: friendships began or were nourished; learning and growth became so immediate that the often-hidden processes were at times palpable.

John Gardner writes in *On Becoming a Novelist*, "In a writer's community, nearly all the talk is about writing. Even if you don't agree with most of what is said, you come to take for granted that no other talk is quite so important. Talk about writing . . . fills you with nervous energy, makes you want to leave the party and go home and write."[1] The conference was simultaneously a break from the work of writing and a spur to create again.

* * *

As I've reflected on highlights, I saved one for last: Scott Russell Sanders's keynote reading on Friday evening. It offered much meaning, only in a way that has been trickier to parse. But I need to try.

Some context: as I've mentioned, Sanders's writing has become important to me since I moved to the Midwest. I find an excuse to teach the exquisite "Buckeye" in nearly all my classes from freshman composition to Advanced Creative Writing. His work guided me as an autistic negotiating the physical and psychic terrains of this place.

I had heard Scott read from his marvelous *A Private History of Awe* in Seattle, and later in Massachusetts from his selected essays *Earth Works*. When I sat down the Friday night of Making Literature, with Scott on my own campus, I expected to hear an essay—fresh, different, perhaps unpublished—on one of his go-to topics, whether the environment, social justice concerns, or some aspect of intentional living. Since the day I'd booked him, I'd been waiting for the moment when he'd take the stage and begin reading, his deeply rooted ethos already apparent, piercing. I would steal glances around the room, see the visible signs of narrative transport taking them to a new place with a master at the helm.

But something else happened. I was quite thrown off. I've been processing the experience, though, and I think I'm coming to appreciate it more.

Here's the thing: he read fiction. Not just a story or novel excerpt, where I may have had time to adjust to a character and voice. He read multiple flash pieces, each in the voice of a different character from a very diverse cast. I couldn't help it: I felt panicky from the beginning.

Yes, I was overtired, overstimulated, and overworked. Yes, there's the autistic tendency to crave the familiar. But more than that: I'd known and loved the voice in his essays; I wanted to bask in it again as I'd done before. Instead I heard not just a different voice, but many, and quickly, up to and including the points of view of animals. It was unpredictable, frenetic.

It was also new and spirited.

But I let my expectations get in the way of experiencing the richness of the moment. I had become the fan who goes to a concert, anticipating his favorite song, but early in the set the singer says, "We're excited to play all new material for you tonight." The fan feels betrayed. That's *his* song. The melody, the instrumentation, the memories associated with the lyrics—the song had become such an entrenched part of his reality that it would be unthinkable for them not to play it, as absurd as Jimmy Buffett forgoing "Margaritaville" in front of ten thousand parrot heads in tropical shirts.

That kind of expectation causes the fan, ironically, to wish away the very elements that produced his favorite song in the first place: the artist's creative drive, autonomy, playfulness, and the sense of not just a single successful project but a career. An artist's sustaining vision requires leaps of faith, some small and some great. Aside from questions of how well the flash pieces worked, I could see that I'd been more or less foolishly opposed to them on principle.

I see the reading in a broader light now, and I admire the leap, which I think is bigger than a writer simply working in a second genre. That, I understand; many of us need the freedom to work in multiple modes, to stretch, refresh our imaginations, break contracts with readers that we never intended to enter into, and give expression to images, characters, or lines that wouldn't work in our old genres. But I think the leap I witnessed was even more important than that; I think it was an act of one who "navigates by estrangement."

Not to take for granted the hard work behind any writing, or to suggest that Sanders has written monolithically in the past—he's published plenty of fiction over the years, including sci-fi and children's books. Yet it would be far less difficult for a septuagenarian to keep with the kind of essays that have brought him fame. But there he was, navigating by estrangement through this risky new project in which each of the tales features a completely different cast of characters. The sampling we heard included a small boy living in rural poverty, then a vastly different piece about a young woman who had joined an Occupy Wall Street protest. And yes, at least one piece was from the point of view of an animal.

This undertaking requires courage for any writer. We can, and should, carefully consider the results in due time (that's premature and unfair at this writing, since I heard only a tiny bit of the overall project in process)—but the gesture itself is admirable and points to a way of regarding the creative life that is instructive. The project required humility. We are a small college that had never hosted Sanders before. He might have read any of his best essays and pleased us exceedingly. The short trip up Interstate 69 from Bloomington might have meant an easy paycheck and a stroke to the ego.

Thankfully, though, Scott Russell Sanders is not that kind of writer. He's a risk-taker and a teacher, and he taught us well. I've heard of venues that contractually obligate a writer to read from the genre for which he or she is most acclaimed. I understand the appeal; one wants to give an audience the best possible experience. But I wonder if we're shortsighted in this, as—to return to a music metaphor—a young listener is short-sighted in wanting only a band's slickly produced greatest hits, a manageable dozen tracks each cut to a sub-four-minute radio edit. I wonder if, from time to time, it's healthy for us to see the artistic life in its fullness, the messy processes enacted—to observe the varieties of risk, reward, failure, success.

A life of integrity honors the process, not merely the result—and so must we, if we are to call our conference "Making Literature." At a student-centered event in particular, I see value in writers modeling work that navigates by estrangement, by investment in the very core of art: the attempt at better understanding the world's unfathomable gradations and better empathizing with its vast variety of inhabitants.

Novelist Richard Powers puts it like this: "Fiction is one long, sensuous derangement of familiarity through altered point of view. How would you recognize your world if it wasn't yours? What might you look and feel like if you weren't you? . . . Fiction plays on that overlap between self-composure and total, alien bewilderment."[2]

I was able to witness a veteran writer set aside familiarity and self-composure to accomplish something that may turn out to be more meaningful than just another great essay. He grappled with the fundamental risks of making literature when there was no need for him to bother. In doing so he showed us a path of unassuming integrity, one that doesn't suddenly end when you've "made it," but continues on.

. . .

If we are to be faithful writers and people, we too can't allow ourselves to stop considering questions like the ones Powers poses: "How would you recognize your world if it wasn't yours? What might you look and feel like if you weren't you?" At every stage we must decide, like Sanders, against resting on our laurels—in the miraculous event that we accomplish anything approaching such a word. If Powers is right, if "only inhabiting another's story can deliver us from certainty," let us take that risk to the very last, for as Anne Lamott has said, "The opposite of faith is not doubt but certainty."[3] Let us take leaps of faith, some small and others large, in our lives and in our work to the end of our days. Let us navigate not by what we think we know but by humble, frightening, beautiful estrangement.

THE TRACKS OF MY TEARS

I was better after I had cried, than before—more sorry, more aware of my own ingratitude, more gentle.

—Pip, in Charles Dickens's *Great Expectations*

Those who do not weep do not see.

—Victor Hugo, *Les Misérables*

In the end, this round of antidepressants didn't do me much good. I tried the latest kind, upped and downed the dose with my doctor, and stuck with the most promising for a year and a half before deciding to ditch them at the end of the summer. Maybe there were days when they evened me out a bit. Though this particular medication has been helpful for others on the spectrum, I'd be trying something else. A good thing, as I had grown tired of the side effects: weight gain, fatigue, insomnia.

And a more sinister development: I couldn't cry.

For a year and a half I could not summon a tear. This, though I endured the death of a beloved family member, celebrations of new births, and a hundred small scenes that may otherwise have prompted wet eyes of sorrow, nostalgia, or joy. Though I don't cry that often, I value the cathartic release when it's necessary.

And I've noticed that for me, it's often connected to prayer. As the Dickens line above suggests, tears can be something of a reset button, grounding our next action in greater compassion. For one who needs all the help he can get, the loss of this gift hurt. Since I could not cry, I felt I could no longer see rightly.

But this story has a hopeful ending: I'm on different meds that dampen both the manic and depressive phases of bipolar. And I've reclaimed the gift of tears. The way recent months have been, I'm thankful—though the tears have shown up much more frequently than before, as if making up for their absence. I'm sure it will even out again, but for now I've coveted each one.

I cried in prayer over the open-heart surgery performed on my friend's six-month-old daughter—and again when I got the news that she had pulled through and was doing well. I cried alone after a student sat in my office, looked out my window at the campus water tower, and told me of personal atrocities she had endured at the hands of an oppressive regime in her home country. I cried sitting next to a recent cancer survivor at a performance of Margaret Edson's play *Wit*.

When my beloved creative writing students came over to watch *Anne of Green Gables*, I found myself crying even though I'd read the book and watched the movie many times. I was caught off guard by one of Matthew's great lines.

Marilla, surprised at the appearance of a girl where a boy was expected, thought immediately of sending Anne away. "What good would she be to us?" she asks her brother.

Matthew quietly turns the tables: "We might be some good to her."

* * *

Yes, I have a sentimental streak a mile wide. But in that moment, Matthew's shifting the focus from his own needs to those of someone far worse off came to stand in my mind for every act of selflessness and grace for which our world is so desperate. In the darkness of my living room, salt streams trickling down my face, I prayed for each one of my students hugging pillows on the couches and floor. I prayed that when things got bad, they could find someone who would be some good to them. I prayed that we'd all decide to be some good to the people around us.

Though I could barely make out the TV screen through blurry eyes, I could see again.

FAMILY AND IDENTITY

I believe that one can never leave home. I believe that one carries the shadows, the dreams, the fears and the dragons of home under one's skin, at the extreme corners of one's eyes and possibly in the gristle of the earlobe.

—Maya Angelou, *Letter to My Daughter*

A TRUE NAME

Man gave names to all the animals
in the beginning, long time ago.

—Bob Dylan, "Man Gave Names
to All the Animals"

He saw that in this dusty and fathomless matter of learning the
true name of each place, thing, and being, the power he wanted
lay like a jewel at the bottom of a dry well. For magic consists
in this, the true naming of a thing.

—Ursula Le Guin, *A Wizard of Earthsea*

On June 16, 1710, a ship dubbed *The James and Elizabeth*
completed its trip from London to New York. Among the German Palatine passengers were Johann Adam Baumann (age
44), his wife Susanna Catharina (age unknown), and their six
children: Margretha Elisabeth (20), Anna Margretha (17), Elisa-
betha Catharina (15), Heinrich Peter (11), Maria Sybilla (9),
and Maria Margretha (7). Several years later, the Baumanns,
along with a small group of fellow Palatine immigrants, became
the first Europeans to settle on the Mohawk River.[1]

A map still exists in which I can see the parcel my ancestors farmed in the town where, nearly three hundred years later, I grew up knowing nothing of the history of my family or its name.

This is not an extraordinary story, not better or worse than anyone else's, nor more important because it happened a while back (by Euro-American standards). It's simply my story, and so I search it out for clues to my identity. The popularity of sites like Ancestry.com suggests a renewed interest in our pasts; many of us are asking, with Juliet: "What's in a name?"

The Bowmans

I have two names now, two ways of being defined: "Bowman" and "autistic." For most of my life I knew only the first, and didn't know it well. Later, I would dream it could be something like *the writer Daniel* Bowman, or *Professor* Bowman. But as a kid, all I knew were my own anxiety-ridden hours.

Growing up, I was the shy, sensitive runt of the litter who felt everything so intensely and couldn't comprehend how others managed to hide their own enormity of emotion. What secret did they understand about how to live? It never occurred to me that they didn't experience the hourly depth of feeling that branded my days, or, more broadly, that there were different ways of being. No one told me that, so I didn't know.

Instead I felt all my wild, extravagant feelings down to the last drop. I laughed until it hurt, I cried at sad commercials on TV, I swung as high as the swing set would go, I climbed to the tops of trees for the rush of looking out. I lived in my imagination, in books, and in the woods. While I played with my brother a lot and cousins on weekends, I felt most at home in my own skin when I was alone.

Two physical factors defined my early years, preventing me from fitting in with others. I seemed marked to be different from the outset, emotionally and bodily, and not in good ways.

First, I had frequent nosebleeds. Sometimes they were a slow trickle I barely perceived until a drop of blood hit the floor in front of me. Other times they were absolute gushers that didn't stop for half an hour. Constant nosebleeds are one of my earliest memories. They happened at home, out playing with the neighborhood kids, at my grandparents' house, wherever. They embarrassed me to no end, making me feel weak and weird.

Second—and much worse—I wet the bed. I suffered from a sleep disorder called a parasomnia, an umbrella term for a number of sleep-related issues. My parasomnia was characterized by unusually deep sleep, where nothing could wake me. I was notorious for sleeping through anything.

Once, when I was eleven, a fatal accident took place in front of our house. A young man led police on a high-speed chase, veered all the way up the steep embankment of our road, and flipped his car, launching it into a lethal arc that ended right in our driveway.

It was a gruesome death. The twenty-nine-year-old's blood and brain matter were splattered on the front end of my dad's 1970s two-tone Volkswagen bus and on the large rocks at the bottom of our driveway, even after the scene was cleaned up.

I slept through the whole thing.

The crash, the ambulance, cops, sirens, my entire family up talking with officers, every light in the house on.

I know the terrible details only from being told about it the next day. Our school bus picked up my brother and me at the bottom of our driveway, precisely where the crash occurred. The stains on the rocks were our constant companion in subsequent weeks. They must've faded after some time, but never in my imagination. My older brother—tough, confident, and well-liked by everyone—was shaken by the event in a way I'd never seen before, and that scared me perhaps most of all. But again, my memory would not be seared with actual images, because I was sound asleep.

I also suffered from night terrors. I would wake with a start, frightened and confused, often in the middle of vivid nightmares, and be unable to talk or respond to voices before falling back into deep sleep. One of the hallmarks of night terrors is having no recollection of them the next day.

Someone, usually my mom, would encounter me in this state once in a while. The next morning, they'd say things like, "I came in to check on you and you sat straight up, looked right at me, didn't say a word, then dropped your head back to your pillow and fell asleep again! Knowing you, you probably don't remember that at all, huh?" Of course I didn't. I hated it. I just wanted to be normal.

I sometimes talked in my sleep. While this is more common, it was still upsetting, especially at friends' houses. It would sometimes become the butt of a joke. I would likely say gibberish or something inconsequential, I never remembered it. But then the next morning—if it were a group of boys—I'd sometimes be picked on, saying I confessed my love for a girl at school or that I was gay or a practitioner of bestiality or whatever disgusting thing they could think up.

(Side note: autistics are generally very trusting, loyal, and tend to take things at face value, so we can be gullible, especially when young. And when twelve-year-old boys sniff out perceived weaknesses like those, they pounce. Therefore autistic kids are regularly picked on and bullied—often by those they consider their best friends.)

And finally, that most humiliating parasomnia of them all: enuresis (loss of bladder control when asleep). This was the source of my greatest shame in childhood. There was no way around it, even when I drank absolutely nothing for hours or tried to set alarms to wake up in the middle of the night and use the bathroom (see "deep sleep" above). I had no access to medical treatment, psychotherapy, or any other tools that might have managed the issue or alleviated my shame. My parents always seemed vaguely annoyed, if not outright angry, about it, or maybe I felt so humiliated that it just seemed to me that everyone else was also embarrassed and frustrated. I was always told I'd "outgrow" it, which didn't happen until I was around twelve and entered puberty.

. . .

Bedwetting was discussed in a 2009 segment on NBC News, and the takeaways were that bedwetting caused extreme humiliation, guilt, and shame. One woman from Georgia who'd dealt with wetting the bed on and off her entire life told the reporter that, at age forty-two, she had still never once discussed the issue with a doctor: "It's just extremely embarrassing to talk about," she said. "I still remember my parents saying it was ridiculous that I would wet the bed, that I was just lazy. I was ashamed about it as a kid."[2]

Elaine Ducharme, a clinical psychologist who has worked with patients with enuresis, says that many people "perceive wetting the bed as being infantile behavior. . . . When you're a child, you're [often] spanked for wetting the bed. It's considered naughty."[3]

Needless to say, engaging in "bad" behavior that cannot be hidden, night after night, year after year, results in deep wells of suffering. Brené Brown defines shame as "the intensely painful . . . experience of believing that we are flawed and therefore unworthy of love and belonging . . . unworthy of connection."[4] Morgane Michael, creator of Small Act Big Impact, says, "Shame is highly correlated to aggression, addiction, depression, suicide, bullying, [and] eating disorders."[5]

Indeed, shame is not an ideal foundation for a childhood—and it has an impact far beyond the early years. Combine bedwetting with all the hallmark features of autism and being constantly misunderstood, and you have a recipe for potential disaster. And that disaster, that misery, was so much of my life. It was a name I kept to myself but knew better than any other.

. . .

Control was an elusive concept in my family life throughout childhood. Our house was in various states of renovation most of the time. After buying a refurbished double-wide trailer on a country road, my parents opted for a proper foundation to be dug and a small addition built off the back. I was eight years old when the construction started, and aspects of the complicated project went on until I moved away to college. Outside and in, certain things were changed or left half-finished, often in a state of flux every few months.

We generally ran out of money before we could make good on whatever part of the project we'd last started. My parents both worked extremely hard—my father making pitchforks and other farming implements at the Union Tool Company in Frankfort, and my mother as a night-shift nurse at Little Falls Hospital—but paychecks only stretched so far when you were raising four kids. Of all the phrases I heard as a child, the most common was, "You can't get blood from a stone."

Before we could complete the exterior of the house with vinyl siding, silver foam board alone covered it for several years. It weathered to an unbearably lonely gray. The bright orange company logo, repeated dozens of times on every board, dulled to something like the burnt yellow pages of old paperbacks. Our roof awaited asphalt shingles for a long time, with only a thin layer of tar paper that would flap when the wind got under it. Oriented strand board comprised the kitchen floor for years. There were holes where old seams didn't line up—when the cellar light was on, you could see into it from above. The kitchen cabinetry had been pulled out in hopes of a remodel. Instead, the plumbing simply remained visible, and the sorts of things that normally go under one's sink were placed elsewhere.

I longed for the stately white clapboard on friends' houses in town, complete with soffit and aluminum flashing, their surname proudly displayed on a mailbox out front. I wasn't ashamed of our family or the house. I wasn't even a social climber wishing for wealth. It was just that I had a name other than Bowman, a name I wouldn't understand for years: autism. I longed for stability, the age-old autistic desire for structure and a corresponding abhorrence of change. I couldn't handle the constant alterations, even if they were positive. I just wanted to feel settled, to *be* settled. With a tumultuous inner life that never let up, the need for a steady outer world to help regulate my emotions was especially insistent.

. . .

And so, as if in a self-fulfilling prophecy, I felt pushed inward. The name "autism" comes from the Greek *autos*, which means "self." The "ism" means "a state of being." So autism connotes "the isolated self"—apropos of the alienation I have spoken of. In many ways, I wholly identify with that connotation. Yet I would like to claim the literal meaning as a new name for what I was and am: the word "autism," in its purest form, actually means "the state of being one's self." There's a larger issue of authenticity here, one that I would need, and still need, to keep living into.

. . .

As a child in search of sanctuary, I turned to the woods. I climbed trees and sat daydreaming in the crooks of branches, comforted by the constancy of a woods that really hadn't changed much since the days of the Iroquois Confederacy. In those woods I sometimes dug up arrowheads of the original inhabitants of the Mohawk Valley—the Mohawks, Oneidas, Onondagas. I built stick forts, swam in Tory Creek, and spent the winter tunneling through the wild drifts of snow. I was happy alone.

I played with my brother a lot, and some of these memories are among my favorites. He taught me things, and I believed in him, his confidence, his vigor. However, I could never understand the ongoing conflict that accompanied and defined us every day. He wanted to compete, constantly and to the exclusion of all else. I wanted to cooperate, to be on the same team working to defeat an invisible enemy. He being two years older and bigger, I couldn't best him in anything anyway and had no desire to—no will to win, no understanding that I was supposed to want to win at things. I just wanted to imagine, to luxuriate in the world of the senses sparked by the woods, the rustling of leaves underfoot and the cool shade of the shagbark hickories and tall maples. The woods were a refuge.

Even when I was with my family, I still liked being outdoors best. I would help as we chopped and stacked firewood to prepare for winter. I gathered seasoned kindling, broke it into fireplace-sized pieces. I helped dig a ditch to reroute the water that flowed off the hill and muddied our gravel driveway. My family and I built up the bank on the roadside with beautiful native pines and their strong root systems—I watched them grow from saplings to mature trees over twenty feet tall. We grew tomatoes in a small garden at the bottom of the back hill. We ran around the field at my grandparents' and ate from the apple and plum trees. We swam in Canadarago Lake; we camped all over the Adirondacks. We often did nothing special, but we did it outside, and I liked that best.

. . .

Back to my surname: Bowman derives from "Baumann," which is a "long-established surname . . . of early medieval German origin, and is either a status name for a small farmer or a nickname meaning 'neighbor, fellow citizen,'" according to the Surname Database.[6] Other sources note that the name has its roots in the Middle High and Old German word *baum*, meaning "tree."

I've come to love the earthy resonance of those etymologies. We have indeed been citizens living in the woods by the trees, first on the banks of Germany's Rhine and then New York's Mohawk River. How did we come by our citizenship? Not unlike my family toiling to make ends meet in the 1980s and '90s, my ancestors' story is also mired in struggle—and gives me more clues about who I am.

The Baumanns

Johann Baumann and Susanna Dresch, the only daughter of a shoemaker, married in Bacharach, Germany, in February 1688. Their native region endured destruction and pillaging from wars waged by the Swedes, the French, and the Saxons. Whichever prince claimed dominion raised taxes, squeezing every penny from the Palatines until the land was wrested from him in the next war.

Then came the winter of 1709, the coldest on record, later called "The Year Europe Froze." Those who had anything left lost it: the grain froze, livestock froze, people froze to death in their beds at night despite building roaring fires before going to sleep. It was said that birds froze in midflight. The city of Paris alone reported a death count of over 24,000.

Across Europe the lack of food and drink caused famine and rioting. As always, the natural disaster hit the poor the hardest. My ancestors were among the most brutalized. *Robinson Crusoe* author Daniel Defoe wrote about them in his *Brief History of the Poor Palatine Refugees*, describing them as one of the lowliest people groups in the Western world at the time. This should have been the end of the story for the Baumanns, as it was for so many thousands just like them. But somehow, they—we—survived.

Europe was at a loss for what to do with the miserable Palatine hangers-on. Queen Anne had an idea. Her colonies in Carolina had been producing pitch from the pine trees to be used by the Royal Navy. She would ship the Palatines to the New World and allow them to pay off their passage by making more pitch.

A master of marketing, she began a campaign, sending a team to the Palatines to start rumors and disperse books with her picture on the cover and the title page in gold letters. The books detailed the attractions of the "Island of Carolina"—foremost being (1) the availability of good farm land and (2) freedom from invaders. Buzz about *The Golden Book* infiltrated the starving Palatinate, encouraging families to leave behind their shambles and strike out for the colonies. I can only imagine the excitement and fear Johann and Susanna Baumann felt upon hearing of this magical place, and leaving home for a new life across the ocean.

The journey began as the ships carried the Palatines down the Rhine to the Dutch city of Rotterdam. The four- to six-week journey was fraught with malnutrition and disease; some died before this first leg was completed. The rest camped outside Rotterdam for weeks—the city could not support them. It was still winter, and the refugees lived in "shacks covered with reeds," according to scholar Henry Jones Jr.[7] The death tolls climbed within the camp.

Survivors eventually sailed from Holland to London, where they were forced again to camp outside the city. A fortunate few received government-issued tents. Even if they survived the elements, however, they were not out of danger: the British citizens resented their presence and its perceived draw on the city's resources. Some Londoners formed a mob and attacked the Palatine refugees with axes, hammers, and scythes, killing many and wounding others.

The Palatines had nothing with which to fight back. How did Johann and Susanna Baumann protect themselves and their children, and thwart death again?

The queen had to act quickly, for she'd become a victim of her own PR blitz. Her first action was to send some of the ships back to Holland and then back to Germany. A deadly round trip for nothing! Other Palatines were dispatched to Ireland and around the UK. The original plan was starting to look disastrous.

Of the 30,000 refugees who left Germany, only about 13,000 made it to England, and only about one-fourth of these ragged, sickly ones finally set sail for America.

. . .

More bad news: for the long transatlantic journey, the Palatines were packed into unsanitary ships infested with vermin. Many became ill and died. Then the entire fleet was ravaged by typhus. More died.

Yet the day finally came when the survivors saw the shores of the New World. Even with that miraculous arrival, though, life did not get easier. British officials had no idea what to do with 2,500 disease-laden German-speaking newcomers. At first they demanded the immigrants camp on an island off the shore of New York City (typhus was still claiming victims after the landing).

Finally the officials had no choice but to accept them. They relocated them up the Hudson and put the healthy to work, making it clear that their indentured servitude would continue for years to come. They broke up families, forced children to work, and generally ran things terribly. To boot, the British didn't understand until then that the northern pines of upstate New York were characteristically different from the pines in Carolina; the New York varieties were, in fact, worthless for the production of pitch. Suddenly, the work that was supposed to have kept the Palatines busy and profit the Crown had disappeared.

Some Palatines staged a revolt, demanding to be free and to receive the land they had been promised from the days of *The Golden Book*. The revolts were put down.

. . .

Back in England, the Tories won control of Parliament from the Whigs, who had sponsored the Palatine relocation. The Tories pulled financial backing from the project they never agreed with in the first place. Officials in the colonies were left to deal with "the Palatine problem" on their own. Their government back home offered no support and even lost interest in the results.

At that point, many Palatine families simply walked away. But a band of about forty families figured that their best shot was still on upstate soil. So they ventured into the wilderness further up the Hudson, to the Mohawk River. The Baumanns were one of these families. The decision to head northwest would profoundly shape my life three hundred years later.

The British tried to discourage the deserters by not allowing them to take any government-owned tools they would need to clear the land. They went anyway and devised their own tools. Accounts show Palatines using tree branches as pitchforks, hollowed-out log ends as shovels, and knotted pieces of wood as mauls—all in the same river valley where my father would later make these implements in a factory to feed our family.

Trees. Baumann: "man of the trees." Citizens, neighbors working the earth together.

. . .

This is no rags-to-riches myth; it's a story of hard work, plain grit, and community. It is worth adding that while the French and British relationship with the Iroquois Confederacy would be marked by bloodshed, the Palatines on the Mohawk River lived in peace with the natives, who helped them survive their first winter.

· · ·

In "The Power of Naming," J. B. Cheaney writes:

> Notice how quickly Adam progresses. From pointing and say-
> ing "elephant," he bursts into poetry when confronted with
> a creature like himself: "This indeed is bone of my bone and
> flesh of my flesh. She shall be called Woman because she was
> taken out of man." He's speaking not only conceptually but
> metaphorically. He's making a clear logical connection, a valid
> comparison. He's not just talking; he's understanding. And
> creating: Out of a cloud of words steps a relationship.[8]

The name of the game for the Palatines was survival, and the
Baumanns were survivors. They were inventive and industrious.
What's in a name? A story of overcoming hardships in pursuit
of a better life, even in the face of outrageous odds that claimed
friends and relations at every step.

I wonder now about my other name, *autistic*. I, too, survived,
only in my case it was a childhood filled with shame and struggle,
often against the limitations of my own body. Autism is genetic,
and, contrary to pseudoscientific YouTube conspiracy theorists
and anti-vaxxers, it's always been with us. I wonder if my ancestors made it in part because of that peculiar autistic brand
of persistence, which has led to many great breakthroughs in
technology, in the arts and humanities, and in the lives of regular
people.

To know who I am, I needed to know the power of our name,
the story of the Palatine immigration, of the Baumanns enduring
during some of the more difficult circumstances any group on
earth had faced. A quick summary would not have sparked my
compassion—would not have caused me to *imagine* my ancestors for any more than a passing moment of intellectual curiosity.

Story holds metaphor, and metaphor enables the creation of
a bond. Adam names the animals with wonderful aplomb, but

when he names his partner, he reorients himself as well. His name stays the same, but its meaning changes in some foundational way. There's a story at that point, one that still moves us today, a story of how people relate to one another and make their way through the world together. As J. B. Cheaney says, "Out of a cloud of words steps a relationship."[9]

Name is related to identity, and identity comes in part from story. When I learned my family stories and, much later, more stories by and about my autistic kin, my neurotribe, around the globe, I could see myself in a new, greater context and enter into relationship—into community—with both the quick and the dead . . . and perhaps most importantly, with myself. I could inhabit a richer understanding of what community means. I could even "burst into poetry" and celebrate my heritage, my name.

. . .

In his essay "Naming and Being," Walker Percy speaks of the namer as making us "co-celebrants of being." He says,

> When a tribesman utters a single word which means the-sun-shining-through-a-hole-in-the-clouds-in-a-certain-way, he is combining the offices of poet and scientist. His fellow tribesmen know what he means. We have no word for it because we have long since analyzed the situation into its component elements. But we need to have a word for it, and it is the office of the poet to give us a word. If he is a good poet and names something which we secretly and privately know but have not named, we rejoice at the naming and say, "Yes! I know what you mean!" Once again we are co-celebrants of being.[10]

Before my autism diagnosis, I had analyzed my childhood "into its component elements," seeing it from my lonely and limited perspective. When I learned the Palatine story, I could celebrate a victory. I'd been named again, with a fuller, more ancient name. And by newly addressing the question "What's in a name?" my ancestral narrative helped me begin addressing that other question that lurks below the surface: "Who am I?" The first question belongs to Juliet; she must know about the power of a name in relation to someone she loves. The second question belongs to Oedipus; he must find the true nature of his being.

"How did my family survive?" is a poignant and interesting inquiry for me, in part because it's a starting point to answering, "How will I go on?" I need more stories in order to answer that question, stories and poems and essays the language of which reflects my autistic humanity back to me across time periods and cultures. I will need new words and, finally, a new name.

In biblical terms, a new name signifies a change in direction, turning away from one thing toward another. Lisa Nichols Hickman reminds us that "God called Abram and Jacob and then named them Abraham and Israel—their names marking a dramatic shift in life's trajectory, a new orientation, a new mission, a new way of life bound in faith to the God who named them."[11] Other examples abound.

In the book of Revelation, God promises, "To the one who is victorious, I will give some of the hidden manna. I will also give that person a white stone with a new name written on it, known only to the one who receives it" (2:17). That's a substantial promise, a name infinitely more meaningful than *Baumann*, its Anglicized form *Bowman*, or even *autistic*; it's a fulfillment, perhaps, of my first name, Daniel, a Hebrew name that means "God is my judge." But what is the judgment?

A name is always a kind of judgment; everyone who learns it will call the named one a certain thing but conceive of the named as a certain *kind* of thing. Something is always lost in that transaction, in part because the name cannot contain all the stories that make the named one everything they really are— the true name—how God sees each of us. A name from God, "known only to the one who receives it" is a strange, thrilling prospect. Perhaps whatever's on that white stone will change what it means to ask "What's in a name?" and two of the significant questions it contains: "Who am I?" and "Who are we?"

. . .

Until then, I am doing what I can to define my earthly names, the only ones I have, for myself and for my own children, who will live in this world as Bowmans. I was among the first in my family to complete a college degree. And now as a professor, I get to speak beauty, truth, and goodness into the lives of many. I'm the faculty sponsor for the campus group Students for Education on Neurodiversity (SEND), whose mission is to "eradicate the stigma around neurodiversity and promote good mental health for all." I believe that in these positions of responsibility, I can help people live into better stories.

With my autism diagnosis, I came to learn much more about what made me tick, what lay beneath the surface. I came to know that my way of being in the world, which made me deeply ashamed throughout my childhood, was not my fault. I came to know that the constellation of traits I displayed had a name: autism—and that taking on the name autistic, while scary, could also be redemptive. In the end, it's about being my true self.

I'm working to create saving stories so my daughter and son can grow up with a fuller understanding of what it means to be a Bowman—so our house will feel like home, and so story and identity can come together in helpful, generative ways for them. But I'm also doing the work of learning and telling old family stories, not as a before to which there's a better after, but as a steady continuum that brings the generations together, a dynamic force that helps us know our names.

LOVING THE EXPANSE

The point of marriage is not to create a quick commonality by tearing down all boundaries; on the contrary, a good marriage is one in which each partner appoints the other to be the guardian of his solitude, and thus they show each other the greatest possible trust. A merging of two people is an impossibility, and where it seems to exist, it is a hemming-in, a mutual consent that robs one party or both parties of their fullest freedom and development. But once the realization is accepted that even between the closest people infinite distances exist, a marvelous living side-by-side can grow up for them, if they succeed in loving the expanse between them, which gives them the possibility of always seeing each other as a whole and before an immense sky. . . . For the more we are, the richer everything we experience is. And those who want to have a deep love in their lives must collect and save for it, and gather honey.

—Rainer Maria Rilke, *Letters to a Young Poet*

On New Year's Eve I had the privilege of attending the wedding of two dear friends in cold, lovely Georgetown, Ontario. I pulled double duty as a groomsman and reader. The passage I read—the one above—surprised me when I first saw it.

I had read Rilke's book of advice when I was young, but I'm sure I arrogantly passed over some of the language about an "expanse" between my beloved and me, and the "impossibility" of merging. I was twenty and in love, and those words didn't account for how I felt. But here was this wonderful couple in Canada—in their late twenties, well-read, self-aware—who had chosen a passage focusing on the distance between them to be read at the very event that would bind them together. What a holy paradox.

I read the passage in the ceremony. And I've contemplated it many times since. I've been meditating on the facts that "even between the closest people infinite distances exist," and that if people can accept such a truth, then "a marvelous living side-by-side can grow up for them, if they succeed in loving the expanse between them, which gives them the possibility of always seeing each other as a whole and before an immense sky."

I've begun to wonder how many of the problems Beth and I have lived through over the years can be traced to my failure to honor, much less love, the expanse between us.

There is a thin line in the autistic life between controlling one's environment for safety and attempting to control the people around you. At my worst, I've tried to change her, to transform her into something I think I need, something much less than the fullness of who she is. That robs her—robs us both, really—of our "freedom and development."

And that robbery is, frankly, nothing short of evil.

If a mixed-neurotype marriage is to flourish, we must continue to grow in our understanding of what the other needs. I've focused a great deal in recent years on learning what I need in order to thrive as an autistic adult who survived an often-difficult childhood. And now I keep returning to the image of Rilke's expanse as a new starting point for understanding Beth's needs as we enter our forties. As her body and mind and heart continue to change. As our kids grow up in the blink of an eye and fight their own battles. Now more than ever, I vow to guard her solitude and trust her.

· · ·

So I think back to New Year's Eve when I celebrated two friends pledging vows. One of those vows was a determination to love the expanse between them.

As I look toward spring, I'm thankful this long winter will be over. I think of the increasing warmth of the sun and the return of living, growing things. Yet I can see that true renaissance—rebirth—will only come into my life if I, too, vow to see Beth each day "as a whole and before an immense sky," and to love the expanse between us.

Let us go forth and gather honey.

PEACE IN TERABITHIA

Blessed are the peacemakers, for they will be called children of God.

—Matthew 5:9

The church needs to be a place where stories are read. The exercise of the imagination is the training ground for compassion. Stories educate the heart. They are vehicles of confession, thanksgiving, and petition.

—Marilyn Chandler McEntyre, *Caring for Words in a Culture of Lies*

I take a seat in the lecture hall at the Efroymson Center for Creative Writing at Butler University in Indianapolis. It's Saturday afternoon, and Una and I are here for her creative writing class. The space is beautiful: a stately old home remodeled and repurposed to serve Butler's MFA program. Canonical and contemporary works line the shelves to my right; I'm in a section of S through W and catch glimpses of Leslie Marmon Silko, Isaac Bashevis Singer, Leo Tolstoy, and Alice Walker. There's also a copy of Chris Ware's acclaimed graphic novel *Jimmy*

Corrigan: The Smartest Kid on Earth, which the *New Yorker* called "the first formal masterpiece of [the] medium."[1]

On a table in the back lie recently published issues of *Booth*, the national literary journal named, I take it, for famed Indianapolis writer Booth Tarkington, one of only three American novelists to win the Pulitzer more than once. (Faulkner and Updike are the others.)

That my daughter is here in this literary center doing creative writing gives me a dual rush of pride and thankfulness. I am, after all, a writer and I teach writing, and her mother is a poet who recently published an excellent debut collection. Watching Una develop a passion for books has been extremely gratifying. She's a great reader, having flown multiple times through nearly every middle-grade novel and series in our town's library, from *Guardians of Ga'Hoole* to Erin Hunter's feline *Warriors*, from *Percy Jackson and the Olympians* to *Harry Potter*.

I'm thankful that stories are helping shape the working out of her faith. I believe Marilyn McEntrye's assertion that stories are "vehicles of confession, thanksgiving, and petition." Literature, it seems to me, is uniquely positioned to foster spiritual growth by nurturing empathy and teaching us to love ourselves and our neighbors better.

I believe that reading helps us develop a sense of God's incarnate love. As an autistic who lacked an intuitive understanding of people, I clung to books to show me the inner workings of others. I became fascinated by what I learned, and it's helped me navigate my life, including marriage and parenting. Before Una was born, I built her a library of the best children's books by scouring thrift stores.

These days we're raising our kids in a poverty-stricken Rust Belt town: unemployment, lack of opportunity, poor health, prevalent drug use, incarceration, and other issues have affected their classmates and neighbors. We desperately need a generation that has the chance to cultivate concern for and sensitivity to the well-being of others, to craft peace where challenge abounds, where brokenness and fear are ubiquitous. I pray that Una's investment in reading and writing will contribute to her burgeoning sense of justice and service.

. . .

One day her reading took a starkly realist turn: she sat down next to me on the couch and cracked open Katherine Paterson's *Bridge to Terabithia*. Beth and I exchanged worried glances. Many of the stories Una has loved are rich and artfully rendered, offering poignant encounters with the self and the Other in various forms. Yet I was scared that the death of a character her own age in *Terabithia* might be too much to handle.

I worried—I who spend my days preaching to students that good art should both "comfort the afflicted *and* afflict the comfortable," should shake us out of our complacency as often as needed (which, it seems to me, is quite often). I who just finished teaching Euripedes's *Medea*, featuring a protagonist who becomes at least as Other, as perfectly challenging for a reader to encounter, as anyone in all of literature. The play is so hard for audiences to reckon with that scholar Emily McDermott subtitled her book-length study of it *The Incarnation of Disorder*.

When it came to my daughter, I wondered if the timing was right to navigate this particular encounter. Late in the book, when Jess's father attempts to comfort Jess upon Leslie's death, he says, simply, "Hell, ain't it?" And the narrator remarks, "It was the kind of thing Jess could hear his father saying to another man." The remark signifies a milestone in Jess's coming of age: his trip to the Underworld, the trip that no quest toward identity, no journey from innocence to experience, can circumvent . . . not even via the protection of a well-meaning parent.

Though it shook her, Una loved the book, and in fact she turned around and read it again straight through. I wanted to ask about it but tried to give her space. I wondered how she experienced the story; I wondered at the forms of her approach toward, and immersion in, this particular encounter—with the characters, with the tragedy, and ultimately with her own mortality.

Arnold Weinstein has written that art and literature "help create denser and more generous lives, lives aware that others are not only other, but are real. In this regard," he says, they add "depth and resonance."[2] If we have any hope of peace—in ourselves, in our families and small private spheres, in our communities—that hope may be inextricably related to our willingness to encounter others. And for those of us who generally lack the resources to trot around the globe, the arts provide the most fertile soil in which encounter can take root. For those who are inclined, flourishing seems more possible.

As I think of the books shelved beside me at Butler, I consider the quality of encounters Una will have when she's ready, from reading Celie's letters to God in *The Color Purple* to learning the traditions of Old World Jews in "The Gentleman from Cracow" to following the eponymous Jimmy Corrigan to Michigan as he seeks to meet his estranged father. Furthermore, I love that she's learning to tell her own stories, to navigate relationships between form and content, to enact love through imaginative "vehicles of confession, thanksgiving, and petition."

As an autistic parent, I've sometimes worried that I lack the resources to give my kids everything they need. How can I show them how to be with others, to live in community, when it doesn't come naturally to me, when my brain wiring isn't quite set up for that? When I muse over the power of story, I'm grateful for all it can do. As it helped me learn about the lives of others, so will it help my kids. I'll keep facilitating that process by giving them books and more books.

* * *

I finally asked Una about *Bridge to Terabithia*, casually, not wanting to push. She told me of the overwhelming sadness. But also, she reminded me of all the good Leslie does for the aching Jess, pointing out that it was Leslie who was new in town and had every right to need lifting up herself. And yet it is she who transforms her pain into blessing. Una pointed out how Jess passes on the boons he receives by making May Belle the new queen of Terabithia at the end.

It was clear that, for her, the story has a lot to show us about connection, healing, and peace, however imperfect—not despite the suffering but because of it.

SPECTRUM INTERVIEWS

INTERVIEW BY MOLLY

Senior at Rutland High School, Vermont

One day I got an email out of the blue from Molly Engels, a high school student doing a research project on autism. She'd read my essays online and asked if I'd be willing to correspond about autism, writing, and life. Most of the time I would probably decline, as writing out responses takes a lot of time and effort. But after looking closely at the compelling questions she asked, I saw the interview as an opportunity. Even as I was helping her conduct research for school, she was providing me with a chance to articulate and elaborate on many autism-related thoughts that had been bouncing around my head. For that, I'm grateful.

Molly Engels (ME): What's your story?

Daniel Bowman (DB): My story is wrapped up in other stories, from Roald Dahl and C. S. Lewis to Charlotte Brontë and contemporary novelists like Elizabeth Strout. I've always been fascinated by language and narrative. Although I grew up in a blue-collar home, I ended up going to college, where I learned how my faith and love of books and writing could come together to form a basis for the kind of life I wanted. So I studied English. I admired Victorian novels, art films, theater, jazz and folk music, and poetry. I went on to get an MA in comparative literature and an MFA in creative writing. My MFA thesis became my first collection of poems, *A Plum Tree in Leatherstocking Country*, which was published by a small press in Chicago.

Being steeped in the arts makes me different from a lot of autistic men, who are better known for interest in STEM subjects. I guess I defy the stereotypes that say autistic guys are numbers savants or computer hackers. One of the reasons I started to write essays about autism is that I discovered that almost no one was writing from the perspective of an artist on the spectrum. And the same goes for those of us working in higher education.

ME: How have you learned to live with autism?

DB: That's simple: I haven't.

I'm not very good at being an adult human in general. My life is, at best, three steps forward, then two steps back. Yes, there's often a net gain (a degree earned, a piece of writing published, a moment where a relationship was well tended to, a successful social interaction), but it comes at a great cost to me and those who try to love me. But I'm forever trying. I learn more about myself and autism and other people every month of every year, through reading and teaching and living in community.

I'm committed to flourishing, for myself and for my family. To me, that means I am committed to reconciling my flawed self to the flawed world in order to serve the common good, starting in my own home and community. (That does *not* mean I'm apologizing for being autistic—in fact, just the opposite.) Ultimately, that is what I believe we all need to do: reconcile our flawed selves to the flawed world. That is a tall order for even the best equipped, even those who've had every advantage. To begin, we must recognize the things we can and cannot control, for example.

To say I'm poorly prepared for this journey is to understate the case. As a follower of Christ, however, I find the grace of God to be a source of strength.

So there we are. I'll get up in the morning tomorrow and try: take carefully planned actions of self-care; routines that enable me to work; steps to being at my best at home and in the world; and counseling to affirm and adjust and learn and grow.

ME: What is the hardest thing that autistic individuals face? How do we as a society become more aware of ways to help?

DB: Well, I can't speak for anyone but myself. And I bear in mind that I'm speaking from a place of certain kinds of privilege, being a white cisgendered male with the ability to speak, not to mention a terminal degree in my field and a tenure-track university professorship. (The word "privilege" here is not a political statement but empirical fact.)

For me, feeling unsafe or on edge or misunderstood or lonely—these are hard things I deal with nearly every day. For others—we know, for instance, that gender and sexual identity are often highly complex among people on the spectrum—these people may literally not be safe from threats or actual assault. Or how about autistic people of color? These are real people who are often vulnerable, marginalized, and have little access to support. Not that it's a suffering contest, but it does behoove one to look around and get context.

For me, a challenge is something as simple as answering the phone. I'm going to do something unusual here and give you a few paragraphs from the novel I'm working on. It's a third-person point of view, and here the narrator is in the heart and mind of the main character, Alex, an autistic high schooler. It's a passage of exposition. I think it illustrates what many of us on the spectrum go through every day:

His mother thought nothing of answering the phone, even before there was caller ID. The intrusion seemed to him so obviously appalling that his mother's attitude in the face of it still startled him every time. She'd answer the damn thing while doing dishes, cranking her neck toward her shoulder to hold up the receiver with no hands. Made no difference to her who was on the other end—a wrong number she shrugged off; a bill collector she handled with dignity and ease (unless it was dinner time; then she might attack); a friend or family member she spoke with effortlessly, somehow knowing when to speak and when to listen, when the conversation had played itself out, when to use a whole complicated array of inflections and intonations in her voice and diction to let someone know she cared, was mad, was pleased, was—well, anything at all. Anything the occasion called for. Every time it happened it seemed to Alex that she'd just fought, and won, an enormous battle. Yet the clash never depleted her. In fact, it was just the opposite: she was energized by it.

For Alex, autism could be felt most fully in the sound of a ring tone and the terror it brought—the fear and indecision, the hundred racing thoughts and feelings.

He would second-guess everything he said on a phone call; stay on too long or try to get off the line too quickly (he never had any idea which was which); talk when he should've just listened and go mute when he was expected to say something; try to conjure a phrase to meet the moment and instead blurt out some awkward approximation. Oh, it was a waking nightmare. Speaking of waking, he would lie in bed that night and replay the call in his mind, thinking of every witty and well-timed thing he should've said. A new cycle of self-loathing would begin and take days to recede. The next day he'd watch a half-hour sitcom where good-looking people with perfect hair would pick up telephones and intuitively deliver every word, every retort, every layer of irony, all in flawless measure, and he would alternate between fascination and despair.

I think the first thing people can do to help is begin learning more about all the variations of human identity. In my case, I'm talking about neurodiversity. What percentage of Americans could even correctly define that term? All of us need to listen to the stories of others, in the interest of gaining insight and coming alongside people to help them and be helped.

A number of my friends know that I'm autistic, but only one or two have read books I recommended that pertain to my experience. They've talked with me about it, and asked me questions, and really listened. That's an act of love so powerful I cannot begin to explain my gratitude. To those friends I'll be devoted forever. They've empowered me toward a creative self-actualization—toward a place where I have something healthy to do with my pain: not merely to transmit it (back onto myself and others) but to transform it.

ME: When you were getting an education, what did you wish was different about how educators treated you? What worked?

DB: Insofar as I can reimagine the past at all, I do see it anew through the lens of autism—with textures and contours I could never have perceived at the time.

I will say this: in education as in life, I have always responded terribly to authoritarians and very well to those who treated me with, to use an old-fashioned word, tenderness.

I had a fifth-grade teacher who came down very hard on anyone who was disorganized. He was from the old school and demanded obedience. One time he walked over to my desk—now, I'm a shy and awkward little ten-year-old, and he's a middle-aged man with gray hair and a beard—and he slammed my desk to the floor with one fell swoop, where it crashed so hard I thought someone had shot me in the head with a rifle. All my worldly belongings spilled everywhere, and the sensory overload, public humiliation, and utter disorientation formed one of the worst experiences of my childhood.

According to his ethos, he thought he was teaching me a lesson: that I would clean out my desk and organize my papers and jump right on the straight and narrow and certainly thank him for it down the line if not sooner. Instead, what he accomplished was bullying and scaring the living hell out of a deeply sensitive child who would forever hate the man's guts, a child who relearned in that moment to distrust on principle all teachers, and by extension all authority figures, and would think himself unworthy of love or even kindness for years after. I was a little runt of an autistic child, and after that my shoulders and head drooped even more than you'd think possible. You could've knocked me over with a feather.

So, you know: don't do that.

On the other hand, when someone has treated me with tenderness—when an educator made even the slightest attempt to understand me or even just give me the benefit of the doubt (and I have always had some teachers like that), I've been fiercely loyal to them. Actual learning can take place then. Gentleness, kindness, sensitivity to the fact that the experience of another person may render their way of being in the world completely different from your own . . . that's what I respond to.

It can be a seemingly small thing: for example, when talking with a group, don't ignore the autistic just because they do not respond with eye contact. People do this all the time and probably don't realize they're doing it. They identify the lack of eye contact as a lack of interest or investment. Autism 101: a lack of eye contact does not signify anything of the sort. Yet, to this day, I'll be hanging out with people, and whoever's speaking will stop including me because I'm not staring into their pupils.

As with all of these questions, my response only covers me. There's a vast range of being along the spectrum. The best way to know where, or how, someone is, is to attend carefully to that one's personhood, to listen, to default to kindness.

ME: What is the world like from an autistic point of view and how can I be sensitive to that?

DB: Well, again, not to get into semantics, but this is important: there is no autistic point of view. There are as many autistic points of view as there are autistic persons. It's a hard truth—many people wish it were easier, but it's simply not.

However, of course one can learn a great deal of the basics about autism through reading and by spending time with autistic people. You'll quickly see the variety of people on the spectrum; you'll notice the way that truths about autism are fluid and dependent upon context. There's no linear progression from "low" to "high" functioning; it's more like an equalizer with many different settings, only instead of bass, treble, mid, tone, and fade, they're autistic traits: stims (amounts and types), communication style (verbal, nonverbal, hyperverbal, etc.), sensory sensitivities and overload thresholds, special interests, and much more.

So if you want to be sensitive to autistic people, first learn some of the foundations from books by clinicians and researchers and also by actual autistic people (read entire books—don't just skim articles, or else you're excusing yourself from the hard work you say you want to do). Learn about the spectrum, about sensory processing, adherence to routines, social interactions, special interests, stimming, meltdowns, and the rest. Then respect the complexities of individuals as you come alongside them.

For me, it's like attempting a foreign language when you're in that country. If you're in a different country and you humbly and curiously soak up their culture, including attempting the language out of respect, most people appreciate that. On the other hand, if you arrogantly assume they speak English and know Americanisms and should cater to you as a customer . . . well, you're not likely to make many friends that way. Same thing in the autism world. People need to be affirmed. People value any effort we make to walk a little while in their shoes.

ME: How has autism helped you succeed?

DB: I suppose the peculiarly autistic form of obsession has pushed me forward. When I get into something, I *really* get into it. When I was younger and new at writing, that "something" was poetry, and my curiosity was insatiable. I read and wrote like crazy, and it turns out that's precisely what a person needs to do to get better at writing.

That single-mindedness can be a gift. When I was in college, I encountered arts and culture very powerfully—I came of age on the stuff. From that point on, almost literally from the first English course I took, I knew I wanted to be a writer and to teach literature and creative writing at a college. I wanted to work at a Christian college, where I could explore and be increased by the fertile connections between art and faith.

I think that, because I'm autistic, there was not as much room for me to wander from my life goal. Although neurodivergence can also come with severe motivation challenges and a million issues that make formal education hard, I stuck with it, for no good reason other than I couldn't think of anything else. There's an illogical persistence. That same impulse has led other autistics to make important scientific and technological discoveries. We tend to keep pushing the boundaries when others give up.

ME: Do you wish that things were different?

DB: Most of the time, yes.

This will upset some autistic self-advocates, but yes, many days I wish that I could just be a regular (neurotypical) person. Autism causes many difficulties in my life. I do believe that I'm on a journey toward integration. But it would be terribly dishonest to pretend that I've come to terms with my autistic life and have made total peace with it. There is goodness in the attempt, but I'm not kidding myself.

Also, perhaps in the future the world will be more willing to meet autistics halfway. That could change my answer significantly.

ME: How did you combat the social differences between yourself and your peers, or were you able to do so?

DB: Since I never had a diagnosis until I was in my thirties, I grew up thinking I was terribly shy to the point where it was debilitating. I was always accused of being "oversensitive," which—in a hard-luck town where men make pitchforks, not poems—means "weak."

Later on, when I came to the arts, I recognized myself in the lives of writers and artists who thought—and felt—deeply. I came to see myself as an artist examining what it means to be human, and that required extraordinary sensitivity. So it became an asset.

Only much later did I discover that my strange constellation of deficits and strengths had a name. Which is not to say that everything about me can be attributed to autism—like everyone, I have some characteristics determined by nurture, not nature. Where I grew up, what my parents and siblings did, and more: that all shapes me too.

ME: What has allowed you to succeed the most?

DB: My family—Beth and the kids. If I were on my own, I'm not sure if I would try very hard. I'd be more inclined to give up when things go badly. But I have to put food on the table, and I get to enjoy this astonishing gift of their company, their marvelous humanity. I also have students and colleagues who I like to think count on me, who I like to believe benefit from my contributions to our campus community. One example is the student group SEND: Students for Education on Neurodiversity. I am faculty sponsor of that group, and I attend most of the open meetings as well as the cabinet meetings, where the club officers plan events. My relationship with those students, many of whom are autistic, motivates me to keep working.

ME: Do you think that you are treated differently than individuals without autism?

DB: The answer has to do with how many people know I'm autistic. Most days, I teach students who don't know I'm autistic; I go into Starbucks where no one knows; I go to the grocery store where no one knows, and so on. No one can treat me differently, because they don't know I'm different . . . unless they pick up on it through my actions.

On the other hand, my good friends do know, and they treat me differently because they've discovered what works for me and what doesn't. They're a blessing from heaven.

Let me give you a quick example: a colleague and I were preparing to lead students on a trip to London over our university's January term (a three-and-a-half-week mini-course). A month in London, Canterbury, Dover, Bath, Edinburgh, Cardiff, and a few other locations. How spectacular! We would be spending time at some of the great cultural and artistic sites of Western heritage, from Westminster Abbey to the Tower of London to the British Museum and Saint Paul's Cathedral.

My colleague, a dear and thoughtful friend, advocated with my university to secure additional funding: he wanted just the two of us to take a short scouting trip to London several months before the student trip.

Why? Because he understands what I need. He knows that it's a common adaptation for autistic people to do a "test run" whenever possible before a complex and potentially challenging event. He knew that I would be empowered to add much greater value (and potentially avoid disaster) on the student trip if given the chance to acclimate myself to the new environment. He knows that, for me, it is not a matter of some common initial discomfort, but could be a serious concern. He thought that my needs were worth fighting for.

Isn't that brilliant? It's a miracle to live and work with someone like that. The vast majority of autistic people who've ever lived have not enjoyed such support, and I don't take it for granted.

ME: If you could share one piece of advice to your younger self, what would it be?

DB: Be yourself. You are enough, despite all evidence to the contrary.

ME: If I am a student looking to become more sensitive toward autism, how should I be more aware?

DB: Read about it, and spend time with autistic people. I'll say it again: don't just read brief online articles, read several books (newer ones) about the autism spectrum, some from actual autistic writers. Read blogs by autistic people. Then hang out with us.

Be patient. Make friends with someone on the spectrum. Go out and do stuff together.

This transcends autism, of course. This is about living in community, being a good citizen of the world.

ME: What is one thing that you wish you could change about the public perception of autism?

DB: There is no one public perception about autism—there are many. Generally speaking, I guess I would want people to be more sympathetic and, finally, empathetic. Start by being unafraid.

Here's the thing: Neurodiversity is real, it's not going away, and people ought to be excited about such a momentous breakthrough. We are unveiling layers of mysteries about what it means to be human.

Don't be scared. Many people default to fear; they feel threatened because things keep getting more complicated, and as a result, maybe they feel disenfranchised or lost. They long for a simpler time, a recognizable time. I get that. The rapid pace at which today's world is changing is enough to scare even the most committed progressive. The word "innocent" goes back to a root that means "not yet hurt" or "not wounded yet." When people long for a simpler time, they're really just saying, this hurts and I wish I could go back to before I was wounded. I understand.

We must recognize and check that fear. Instead, let's be curious; let's be in awe of how complex we all are. Let's get excited when the frontiers of knowledge open up even just a little. And let's be aware of what it means: that for the first time in human history, a certain group of people have a better chance to be understood and affirmed and to get what they need in order to flourish and contribute to the flourishing of the culture. That's a wonderful thing.

INTERVIEW BY JENNA

Writer, Mom, and Creator of
Learn from Autistics

Jenna Gensic is a writer, a mom to an autistic child, and the creator of Learn from Autistics: Connecting Parents and Caregivers with Autistic Voices. I was thrilled when she reached out to me for an interview. At her website learnfromautistics.com, she describes her unique mission:

> Learn from Autistics is founded on the following core beliefs:
>
> - Listening to what autistics have to say is valuable.
> - Embracing and teaching neurodiversity is a key strategy to improving the lives of many autistics.
> - There are concrete ways society can help improve the lives of autistic individuals.
> - Promoting acceptance and respecting the dignity of *all* people is beneficial to *all* of society.[1]

Jenna Gensic (JG): Describe your typical teaching day. What are the most stressful and most fulfilling parts of your work?

Daniel Bowman (DB): I teach between one and three classes a day, almost all writing. I also teach a course called Literary Editing and Publishing, where we create *Relief* journal, a national literary magazine that comes out every spring.

Aside from teaching, I meet with students; serve on committees that conduct the business of the university; and sometimes work on my own writing projects, although that's rare between 8 a.m. and 5 p.m.

The most fulfilling parts of my work? First is the privilege of coming alongside talented students who are learning a love for books and writing at a new, higher level. Not a semester goes by when I don't work with very bright students who are delightful people. Since we're in an isolated location, we tend to build a strong, supportive community based on our faith, our love for the arts, and a sense of what we sometimes call "flourishing."

Aside from students, I also have some colleagues with whom my family has become very close. We have dinners together on weekends; we talk about what we're reading and watching and listening to; our kids run around together; we go to church on Sundays. It's a rare gift. For me, teaching in the Christian liberal arts college setting is not so much a job as a lifestyle.

In terms of challenges: a huge stressor on the job, common with autism, is executive dysfunction. Much of college, for both students and professors, is managing dozens of small tasks every day, juggling emails and meeting invitations and grading and class prep and much more, all of which is constantly fluctuating. The people who juggle these things the best win the game.

I struggle with this juggling every single day and miss something a few times a month. Sometimes failing is enough to throw me into a spiral of frustration and depression. My brain will just never work that way, will never smoothly navigate time management, planning, monitoring many tasks, giving attention and focus, problem solving, and other factors we call executive functioning. So people will sometimes mistake me for being lazy, disorganized, or maybe just not that smart. It hurts.

JG: You've written in an essay that it's hard to relax in social situations. Are there ways that others around you can behave that might help lessen this anxiety?

DB: Autism makes it hard to negotiate certain kinds of social circumstances, like attending an event with a lot of people, or a smaller gathering with at least some people whom I don't know. Other times, a gathering even of close friends can become stressful if something unexpected occurs, like someone suddenly decides in the middle of a party, okay now we're going to sing songs or play a board game or whatever. I don't like sudden changes. I will panic. So it's helpful to know about them earlier: "Hey, just so everyone knows, we were thinking about playing guitars later on, after dinner." Then I can make the mental adjustment.

Another thing that's helpful is to be clear during conversation. In response to a question like, "Should we play a board game now?" an allistic person might say, "Um, yeah, I mean, like, we totally *could* do that, I guess." And you're supposed to understand that, pretty much, no, that person is not enthused about the prospects of a board game. But I may be too stressed, or more likely my senses may be too overloaded, to pick up on the meaning of the nonverbal signals and evasive answer. I generally wish to hear just a friendly yes or no so it's clear where people stand.

I've talked about this before, too, but I'll say it again: please include autistic people in the conversation, in the emotion of the exchange, even if they can't sustain eye contact. I get dropped in a conversation, even among close friends, because to their minds I'm not reciprocating their emotion, not connecting with them or what they're saying. So it's almost like their brains send a signal, "Well, he's clearly not paying attention here, so I'll focus on the other people at the table." And they don't look at me again. Then I really *do* tune out, and often walk away, because I'm being left out at that point.

JG: What do you do to relax at home?

DB: I have routines for alone time that I adhere to rather strictly. When I get home for the day, I absolutely need to relax alone for a bit, to recharge. I like to watch a certain sports talk show and eat a snack (I'm trying, and failing, to cut down on potato chips and eat carrot sticks or other healthy foods instead).

I try to jog on the treadmill or take walks in the neighborhood a few times a week, but that falls by the wayside when I get buried in the busyness of the semester. I read a little most evenings (normally literary fiction) and listen to audiobooks (also literary fiction) on my headphones when I'm doing dishes.

Once I've gotten some alone time: I spend time with Beth and the kids, especially on weekends and especially when we can be outdoors. My family likes to hike and be in nature. On school nights, we'll usually watch part of a movie before bed. Other times, my daughter will have a concert or recital or my son will have a game, or we'll all go to a play together. My family likes the theater, especially musicals. Often on weekends, we'll have an evening with friends.

JG: You begin one essay with, "I am autistic. And I am ready to write about it." How did you become ready? What inspired you to share your experiences with the world in this way?

DB: I definitely *wasn't* ready in the sense that I knew what I was about and how to tell that story. The story itself was barely taking shape. I was new to it, and it scared me. So I willed myself to claim it and start writing about it not because I was truly ready but so that—in the act of writing—I could become ready. I could explore and examine and learn and grow in it. Discovery is a function of writing, at least for people who write from places of vulnerability.

Also, I wanted to add another image of autism to the popular imagination. I had only seen autism associated with computer hackers, *Rain Man*, and scientists like Temple Grandin. I wanted to show people that you can be autistic and be a creative writer, an artist. It's the old idea of representation: "If you can see it, you can be it." I want autistic kids who wish to paint or make movies or write novels to see that it's possible. The ways we do those things will be different, but those things are possibilities for us.

JG: What mistakes do neurotypical autism advocates make?

DB: The number one mistake, I think, is not listening to autistic people.

This can take a lot of forms: among the worst, maybe, is people exploiting their autistic children, co-opting their stories for personal gain. We've seen a lot of this.

Don't tell stories that aren't yours to tell. It's okay for parents to share their experiences, but where it goes off the rails for me is when (1) they share intimate details of their children's lives without permission or (2) they more or less pretend that they get it. They don't.

On Twitter, we call it the #OwnVoices movement. If I want to best understand the mood among the people of El Salvador during the revolt against the presidency of José María Lemus, I don't want to read accounts from white Americans who aren't from there. I would rather read the poems of the exiled activist Roque Dalton, one of Latin America's finest twentieth-century poets, or the works of another #OwnVoices writer.

I hope that people afford the same status to autism someday—that they'll seek out our stories first and foremost. As we say: "Nothing about us without us." Yet critics still regularly dole out accolades to allistic people attempting to write the autistic experience.

There's also an argument about how to describe autistic people. Do you say "person with autism" (so-called person-first language) or "autistic" (identity-first language)? The vast majority of autistic people I know—and notice how I said *autistic people*—prefer and indeed fight for identity-first language. Our autism is our operating system, not a flaw that a "normal" me is trapped beneath.

Yet I've seen, too many times to count, a neurotypical on social media attempt to correct an autistic on identity-first language. Part of this is due to the influence of the big corporate autism "awareness" organizations, like Autism Speaks, who historically have not listened to autistic adults.

As I've said elsewhere, the best way to know where, or how, someone is—autistic or otherwise—is to attend carefully to that one's personhood, to listen, to default to humility and kindness.

INTERVIEW BY BRIAN

Pastor in Boise, Idaho

I made a new friend online, a pastor in Boise. He told me that not having read much poetry represented a "defect" in his "education and soul." I was amazed at this beautiful remark, thrilled that anyone, especially a pastor, might think this way. For much of my church life, if there were artists at all, they were, like me, on the fringes, as far from the pulpit as possible. So I have a special reserve of love and respect for that rare species: the pastor shaped by God's truths as found in literature, music, theater, film, visual art.

Some weeks later, Brian and I began messaging about autism. He had read my essays and wanted to learn more, so he asked me great questions. This interaction, and Brian's generous spirit, have been a boon; I wish to reply in kind with the gift of carefully crafted responses.

Brian (B): Are the effects of autism constant or varied? Do you feel as you described in your essays in all conversations or social situations, or does it fluctuate?

Daniel Bowman (DB): The effects *are* constant but, for me, not at maximum intensity every moment. They can be thrown into maximum intensity instantly, though, through any number of factors I can't control: a change in temperature or lighting, a food texture that disagrees with me in the middle of a dinner with friends, an unexpected turn in the conversation, a crowd suddenly showing up where I am.

My experience is certainly mixed at any given moment: in the same breath, I can both charm and upset someone without trying to do either. An autistic friend recently wrote in a Facebook post that she caused confusion in people because they notice in her, even within a single interaction, both socially admirable characteristics and stigmatized ones.

My own traits are best managed when I feel safe.

B: Social situations are clearly difficult. To what extent do you desire them? Are they something you wish for, despite the difficulty, or would you rather avoid them altogether?

DB: This is a complicated question. It's a spectrum, and certainly some autistic people spend a great deal more time alone than others. For me, I need and want friendship, communication, social interaction, affirmation, and fun pretty often. It's just that my participation in those realms is challenging, and I tend to prefer it in small doses. Generally social interaction is not a question of *if* but *how*.

The central concern for me is always: do I feel safe?

I'm talking about a foundational safety. Everyone needs to feel safe in order to thrive relationally—we all understand some form of Maslow's hierarchy of needs—you can't get to real personal growth, creativity, spontaneity, and self-actualization without a basic sense of security. The pyramid is, I think, amplified dramatically for many of us on the spectrum.

I was recently rereading the frame story of *One Thousand and One Nights*, and I was struck by the declaration King Shahryar makes when he discovers his wife's infidelity. This is the very first line he utters to his brother: "No one is safe in this world."

He had the rug pulled out from under him. It seems that the removal of a safe, predictable environment (combined with pride, fury, madness, or other factors) is what catalyzes one of the most violent, misogynistic rampages in all of literature. The king goes on to "marry" a virgin each evening, then have her murdered in the morning. This is his insane version of taking control and bringing about order. Until the genius Scheherazade breaks the game, it plays out with deadly results every night, a consequence in ever-increasing disproportion to the inciting incident.

(I hope it's obvious that I'm *not* saying autistic people are prone to violence, as some media outlets have posited in recent years. I'm merely pointing to an example from literature that demonstrates how a lack of safety and security disorders the soul.)

Scheherazade's brilliance as a storyteller is not just her cliffhanger technique, but rather that, by the very act of carefully developing a narrative arc, she is restoring *meaningful* order in a situation that is extreme. Her stories reintroduce nuance, humor, and an appropriately complex moral feature to an environment in desperate need of a baseline of safety. Through the process of storytelling, she saves herself, the young women of the kingdom, and ultimately the maniacal king as well—not merely staying his hand but in fact, it could be argued, healing him.

It's a profound exchange, and instructive to me. The routines I cling to, and the narrative I shape, are like Scheherazade's stories, assuaging my fears and bringing about order.

If I'm out of my beloved routines, I will likely be off in any ensuing communication. I'm with people all day, and many of those interactions cause stress (both good stress and bad stress). I like to come home and unwind alone. I take off my suit coat, replace it with a ragged twenty-year-old flannel shirt. I turn off the overhead light—too bright, too like the fluorescent lights of classrooms—in favor of the muted glow of the end-table lamp. I account for the little piles of clutter, inevitable in a bustling house. I grab a snack and drink and put my feet up on the coffee table. I try to minimize interruptions.

If I can't create this scenario or some approximation of it for thirty minutes or so, I will not feel safe. If I *can* preserve this routine in some form, I will probably do okay if there's an event on the calendar that night. But I need to live out my small story of comfort, order, and safety first. (In my rigid reliance on routines, I sometimes feel like Tevye in *Fiddler on the Roof*: "And how do we keep our balance? That I can tell you in one word: tradition!")

I feel safe (even around new people) when I'm at a place I've been before—maybe a restaurant where I know the food is good and know where I like to sit and know where to park. This is especially relevant if the situation includes unwritten rules of propriety, as many do.

I remember attending my first classical music concert in college. I had no idea that one piece of music might contain multiple *movements* and that to clap between movements was a faux pas marking you as green, uncultured. One had to wait for the entire piece to be completed before clapping. Suddenly I was on edge, wondering if there were other rules. I could no longer be in the moment, enjoying the company of friends and the music itself. I didn't feel safe. It's a small thing, but that's the sort of stuff that induces stress and can cause me to shut down.

I feel safe when an environment is methodical, because of my hypersensitivities in processing input such as lighting, noise, and the overall tidiness of a space. I feel safe when I'm in a group with one or two people who know me really well, people I can turn to and know I'll be understood. I feel safe when I'm in a group with one or two people who are perennial winners at the social game, who take the pressure off me to perform, to be funny, to correctly intuit which layer of irony we're on now and never fall back a step. (However, there's a thin line between the socialite who makes me feel comfortable and the extrovert who dominates—the latter makes me feel unsafe, unhappy, angry.)

I like knowing how long an event will go on for. I like to understand what time people are coming and leaving. I like to know, if possible, who will be there and even how people will be dressed, if that's relevant. Essentially: anything I can know ahead of time will help. Before any type of new event, you'll see me online, checking the website of the place, any existing reviews that might offer clues into the experience, a map of how to get there, and whatever bits of additional information I can gather.

In a sense, I live a double life. While there are instances in which I can be fully present, I'm always working to stay attuned to my own physiological and emotional responses moment by moment, ensuring my safety—or if safety cannot be attained, managing symptoms until I can get out. The people I envy are often not the smartest or most accomplished; no, the ones who amaze me are those who can do the impossible: be a little carefree, happy-go-lucky.

I would give a great deal to possess a tiny fraction of such a temperament.

B: If we were speaking face-to-face, how should I adjust for autism? What would best enable you to enjoy the conversation?

DB: I'll answer in two ways—the first one is fairly straightforward, I think, while the second is more involved.

My first reaction is this: please include me. Don't mistake my fidgeting and lack of eye contact for disinterest. Many neuro-typical/allistic people have what I've come to consider a terribly ableist habit, and I've been on the receiving end many times: when there are several of us in conversation, the speaker looks to other allistics in the room for traditional affirmation (eye contact at all the "right" times), and once he or she gets it, I get cut out.

The allistics intuit what the speaker wants, and provide it. I do not. I can't. And as soon as I don't, the speaker begins addressing only them, never looking at or including me again, even though I'm sitting right there doing my autistic best to show my interest: leaning in, nodding, making sounds of approval and interest. Please don't expect everyone to play by neurotypical rules of engagement. Don't punish us for our inability to do so. Instead, consider extending some grace—meeting us halfway. We could sure use it. Though we might look "normal," many of us are made to feel wholly Other every day.

Also, it would be tremendously helpful if more people took an interest in learning about the experience of autism, as you have done by interviewing me. I would be thrilled if people began to consider the idea of neurodiversity. I think it's a helpful paradigm as it highlights the inherent created dignity of the autistic mind. The neurodiversity model, in a nutshell, embraces the differences made possible by neurobiological distinctions, understanding autistic brain wiring as a naturally occurring variation and even a potential asset rather than always and only a liability. This view can help eliminate some of the stigma attached to autism and cut into ableist notions of superiority.

Thomas Armstrong, executive director of the American Institute for Learning and Human Development, sees potential for neurodiversity to help create social transformation. He writes:

Instead of regarding . . . portions of the American public as suffering from deficit, disease, or dysfunction in their mental processing, neurodiversity suggests that we instead speak about differences in cognitive functioning. Just as we talk about differences in biodiversity and cultural diversity, we need to start using the same kind of thinking in talking about brain differences. We don't pathologize a calla lily for not having petals (e.g., petal deficit disorder), nor do we diagnose an individual with brown skin as suffering from a "pigmentation dysfunction." Similarly, we ought not to pathologize individuals who have different ways of thinking, relating, attending, and learning.[1]

Armstrong also acknowledges the limits of a neurodiversity paradigm, saying plainly that "success in life is based on adapting one's brain to . . . the surrounding environment. . . . This means that a dyslexic person needs to learn how to read, an autistic individual needs to learn how to relate to others socially, a schizophrenic individual needs to think more rationally and so forth."[2]

I'm drawn to this balanced view. I will continue learning how to make choices that can help me manage and even leverage my autism, honing its positives and minimizing situations that create disturbances for me. But I would like to be better understood.

*   *   *

Brian ended our correspondence with remarks that were deeply encouraging and provide a great example for any fruitful conversation. He wrote: "Thanks for writing these essays; for being brave. I found them very helpful. I don't have much exposure to autism, but I want to understand. Also, maybe these are not even the right questions. Please forgive me if they're not, and help me ask better ones."

They were good questions. I feel honored to be asked anything at all.

I have great hope for the future of the church when I find ministers attuned to the arts and to diversity, as I see that such attention leads them toward empathy.

 NEW
DIRECTIONS

Only the wounded physician heals.
  —Carl Jung, *Memories, Dreams,*
             Reflections

The minister who has come to terms with his own loneliness and is at home in his own house is a host who offers hospitality to his guests. He gives them a friendly space, where they may feel free to come and go, to be close and distant, to rest and to play, to talk and to be silent, to eat and to fast. The paradox indeed is that hospitality asks for the creation of an empty space where the guest can find his own soul.

        —Henri Nouwen, *The Wounded Healer*

FALLING AND AUTISTIC REPRESENTATION

Around the time the new autism minor was announced, my university's theater department staged Deanna Jent's *Falling*, a play featuring an autistic character. I didn't go because I don't think I have any more patience for works about autism written by neurotypical authors. I've been on the #OwnVoices train for a while now, and I'm angry at the literary world for privileging neurotypical voices writing about autism.

It's clear that neurotypical audiences are fascinated with autistic characters. Shows like *The Good Doctor*, *The Big Bang Theory*, *Atypical*, and *Love on the Spectrum* are popular. The problem is: most of those depictions, and the majority of others, are written by and for neurotypicals, in ways they can comfortably digest, in ways that often play to simplistic clichés while centering neurotypical pain, inconvenience, and other reactions to autistic lives.

In part through these pop culture signifiers and tropes, many come to a skewed and sometimes even grotesque understanding of autism. We're seen as the butt of gags, or clueless robots incapable of relationship, or smart but inept fools bumbling through the world, leaving a path of social destruction in our wake. These images creep into the popular imagination and negatively impact our lives.

Autistic writer Katherine May took on this issue in her essay "Autism from the Inside," published in *Aeon* magazine. She describes a meeting with colleagues where the topic of discussion is the long hours of the Silicon Valley work culture.

One person in the meeting, not knowing Katherine is on the spectrum, says that the problem is the tech giants are "institutionally autistic." She is floored by the remark and decides to confront him. She reveals that she is autistic, and asks him to explain himself.

> "I mean," he said, a little more carefully, "that these companies are run by men who probably have Asperger syndrome." A pause. I raise my eyebrows. "And so there's a lack of . . . emotional understanding."
>
> It's hard to imagine any other situation in which a group of educated, liberal adults would conjure a marginalised group as a shorthand for awful. Imagine describing an organisation as institutionally black, institutionally female or institutionally Muslim. Yet, somehow, intelligent people can drop "autistic" into conversation whenever they want to draw a contrast between the unfeeling, insensitive, uncreative parts of this world, and their bright, emotional, magnificent selves.[1]

Of course she's right: the reductive practice of speaking over an entire people group is not tolerated in any other sphere of diversity. And yet the most woke among us accept, embrace, and even celebrate reducing autistic people to a stereotype. Many of these stereotypes come from non-#OwnVoices depictions in books, film, television, and theater.

Hence, my being put off by the play *Falling*.

. . .

#OwnVoices is more complicated than the pen being in the correct person's hand. It's the fact that autistic writers write autism differently because our brains work differently. Our stories reflect those differences. If other stories contain autistic characters but do not reflect the true inner lives of autistic people, then they are false and even dangerous.

I recently completed a draft of a young adult novel called *The Autism Journals*. Several neurotypical readers have told me that they'd like to see faster pacing in the first half. They want more dramatic plot points.

That's fair. Yet my autistic main character experiences small, everyday moments as dramatic (and even traumatic) plot points. For example, someone comes to the house when he's out running errands, and he walks in the door to find them sitting in his seat. That is a moment of excruciating discomfort, and it invariably becomes the major psychological, emotional, and physical event of the scene. The unease sets in immediately and threatens to ruin anything good that was happening.

But in a neurotypical reading, the scene will seem ordinary and unworthy of consideration. Where's the dead body and duffel bag full of cash? Where's the car chase? The sexy seduction? The "normal" stuff? A truly autistic narrative, and character, feels strangely out of sync with their expectations.

Neurotypicals have seen us portrayed as savant geniuses; nerds rambling on about theoretical physics; or objects of hatred, pity, and mystery . . . the cause of ruination of the lives of otherwise decent people.

These last depictions are often surrounded by words like "frank" and "brave," because the authors feel courageous in scapegoating autistics, misunderstanding and misconstruing our meltdowns, defining us by our worst moments, talking over nonverbal people, making the story about their own suffering, and, finally, profiting from the whole enterprise.

If you think I'm exaggerating, read about the play *All in a Row*, which premiered in London in 2019. The main character, a young man on the spectrum, was played by . . . a puppet. Yes, the neurotypical director viewed the autistic character Laurence as so alien, so nonhuman, that he could not even be portrayed by a flesh-and-blood creature.

Director Stephen Unwin wrote a harsh takedown of the play for suggesting that the family's problems are Laurence's fault. He writes, "It's this sense of self-pitying exceptionalism which I think makes *All in a Row* so misguided and, frankly, so dangerous. The great fight for dignity, decency and fundamental rights for people with . . . disabilities must be rooted in the deepest sense of our shared humanity. Autistic people with high needs are our brothers and sisters, our mothers and fathers, they are ourselves. But if we present them . . . as a bomb that threatens our sanity, our family life, our capacity for love, they will inevitably end up being abused, neglected and forgotten."[2]

Amen.

And yet those very presentations—as bombs that threaten the good neurotypical life—are apparently still entertaining plot devices to neurotypicals, and, for now, they still define much of the extent to which neurotypicals will accommodate our stories.

Katherine May makes the point more succinctly:

When I come across instances of this folk understanding of autism, I am reminded of Edward Said's 1978 description of the orientalist gaze, in which the exoticised subjects endure a kind of fascinated scrutiny, and are then rendered "without depth, in swollen detail." Never allowed to speak for themselves, their behaviours are itemised, but not actually understood. The observer, meanwhile, is assumed to be neutral, authoritative and wise. This creates a simulacrum of the Orient, packaged for the consumption of the West. . . . The literary trope of autism has that same kind of memetic contagion.[3]

Thankfully, the impact of *Falling* on our campus would not be entirely negative, would not be entirely packaged for the consumption of the neurotypical majority. In fact in the end, I myself would have the chance to help shape the understanding of at least a few people. I'm reminded of the great Mister Rogers line: "When I was a boy and I would see scary things . . . my mother would say to me, 'Look for the helpers. You will always find people who are helping.'"[4]

I have always found people who are helping me: the colleague who pointed out to me the write-up of the new minor in the campus paper because she knew I would want to see and address it. Another colleague who advocated for a scouting trip to London for my benefit. The friend who asked me to speak in the Identity Intersections series.

And now another: a friend who planned to attend the theater talk-back session about *Falling* and asked me if I was going. I said no, I hadn't viewed the play, and suggested why I wasn't comfortable with it. She paused, then said, "I feel very strongly that we need you on the panel at the talk-back. There's no autistic representation, and that's not okay."

She asked me if I'd be open to her mentioning it to the folks planning the session. I said okay. Within twenty-four hours, the director and the others in charge warmly invited me to speak. I said I would read the script to have a basic grasp of the play, but probably just talk from my own experience.

I will not rehash the entire discussion here. I'll just say this: the moment I began to talk, the energy in the room underwent a profound change. It wasn't because I'm a magnetic figure or dynamic public speaker. It was, I think, because everyone suddenly knew that they would get the inside scoop. They intuited the value of #OwnVoices. I don't know if a group has ever listened to me so intently as people did that afternoon. I felt honored.

The other panelists included the director of the play and the psychology professor who had spearheaded the new minor in autism studies. But as the audience heard me articulate the daily experience of navigating the world as autistic, they began to ask more questions about me than the play.

The experience filled me with hope for the future of neuro-diversity. May many more conversations about autism center the experiences of autistic people so that we can move forward in community, loving each other better.

THEREFORE LET US KEEP THE FEAST

Glimpses of the Labyrinth

Mentoring, at its core, guarantees young people that there is someone who cares about them.

—MENTOR: The National Mentoring Partnership

Joseph Campbell wrote of the archetypal heroic journey, "We have not even to risk the adventure alone, for the heroes of all time have gone before us—the labyrinth is thoroughly known."[1] My mentors went before me, completing their journeys by helping me start mine, giving me glimpses of the labyrinth. They returned home to impart the wisdom they'd earned. They hazarded to pray, to care, to love.

And now I want to take everything I've learned, every battle I've fought, and offer it to the students I mentor—some of whom you'll meet in a moment.

First, I wish to give thanks. Here is a short essay on the beauty and power of mentoring, disguised as a letter to two of my mentors, Michael Landrum and John Leax.

Dear Mike and Jack,

As always, the most recent notes you each wrote me were a boon. I need to begin by thanking you. It's not everyone who has people writing to them at all, much less writing loving and insightful words.

Also as always, I'm sorry I haven't gotten back to you yet. There's no excuse, but there's an explanation, one of the best kinds, at once simple and profound: it's because I'm living the life you made possible for me.

I'm writing books, reading, watching films, teaching at a university, having coffee with students (passing on, I hope, some small part of the grace you passed on to me), traveling, giving readings at conferences, making a literary journal, and more. I'm growing and tending to the growth of others. I'm managing the gifts and challenges of autism as best I can, asking forgiveness when I fail, and failing better.

Aside from the ennui that plagues many writer types from time to time, I love this life. I have for over a decade now. You know too well that I dreamed of just this. In the Mohawk Valley—harangued even in spring by lake-effect snow—on a hilltop family farm, I have heard someone utter the phrase, "Happy as a pig in mud." (Only they didn't say "mud.") Well.

To put it more elegantly, as befits our relationship: a twenty-six-year-old Vincent Van Gogh wrote in a tortured letter to his brother Theo (that I'd be willing to bet you've both read): "Someone has a great fire in his soul and nobody ever comes to warm themselves at it, and passers-by see nothing but a little smoke at the top of the chimney."

How I offered you the pathetic coals of such a fire in me those many years ago. At the time I couldn't stand *time*, its tiny evolutions. I thought I wanted—even deserved—a grand entrance into the world. Fool as I was, you welcomed me.

Van Gogh's letter is about finding purpose. As I listen to my life—as Frederick Buechner, a favorite of you both, urged us to do—I hear purpose in every moment, including, and perhaps especially, the quotidian ones. How else could a man with a taste for the finer things live in a cornfield and be as pleased as that pig? And now I think of another pig, Galway Kinnell's in "Saint Francis and the Sow," how "sometimes it is necessary / to reteach a thing its loveliness . . . / until it flowers again from within, of self-blessing." What did you do in my fiery youth but retell me that, behold, the kingdom of heaven is at hand, until I could flower from within?

Beth and I are doing our best with our two wonderful kids. I'll tell you more about them privately. For now let me say I pray that—to invoke a word that has become important to me—I'm tender toward them, as you were tender toward me. Though I was eighteen (Mike) and twenty-five (Jack) when we met, my heart carried childhood hurts, the kind that can kill you or, sometimes, by miracles, become a great strength if you happen into a way to transform them—a way like art. That transformative power comes through the hands of wounded healers. It was my only chance. Somehow it happened to me through you. I don't ever forget it.

People use the militaristic phrase "above and beyond the call of duty" in reference to those making great efforts on behalf of others. The words apply to the *how* of your care for me, though their context is ironic: I think of you both not in wartime terms but rather as peacemakers in the way of Jesus of Nazareth. In his book *Refractions*, Makoto Fujimura points out, "The Greek word for peacemakers is *eirene-poios*, which can be interpreted as 'peace poets,' suggesting that peace is a thing to be crafted or made. In such a definition, peace . . . is not simply an absence of war but a thriving in our lives."[2] You are peace poets who crafted thriving for me when you didn't need to.

Mike, you taught music courses and piano lessons at Roberts Wesleyan College, playing gigs around the country as a solo performer and with ensembles. Many a time I walked by your studio in Cox Hall and heard you rehearsing. I was not a piano performance major or minor, nor did I have anything to do with formal music training. Yet the most scrupulous accountant could not put a price tag on all you invested in me, frankly with no evidence of future returns. How many times did we eat moussaka or souvlaki at Aladdin's on Monroe Avenue (or our buffet lunches at Tandoor), then see an indie film at the Little or the Dryden and have coffee and decadent tiramisu at Phillips European after? I was always broke, and for the sake of my pride you'd let me contribute my widow's mite and quietly take care of the rest.

But obviously this is not about money. We spent hours quietly perusing fifty-cent paperbacks at Brown Bag Books and Rick's Recycled Books and other places I think are no longer in business. When we were feeling especially inspired, we'd head to the giant Barnes & Noble in Pittsford and I'd take the escalator upstairs to the poetry section. And the CDs . . . we listened to so many back when Borders in Henrietta was open with its glorious music section. Many nights, heading to a movie or a concert downtown or on the folk circuit at Twelve Corners in Brighton, you would introduce me to something I hadn't heard, anything from Streisand singing Rodgers and Hammerstein to the latest Black Rebel Motorcycle Club to the Emerson String Quartet performing Shostakovich.

We saw Joni Mitchell and Bob Dylan on tour together! That alone would be enough.

You shaped me through, as poet William Stafford put it, "millions of intricate moves," which is, by the way, how he described achieving *justice*, something the likes of which my soul knows through your influence.

Jack: not only was I not a major at your college, I wasn't even matriculated! I showed up at your door with nothing but a half-baked dream of poetry. As a graduate student in Cincinnati, though I made a few friends and enjoyed the town, I found myself starved for the ineffable, the spiritual that seemed to seep out of my life in the exacting light of postmodern critique. I felt a longing for some fresh way forward, a third way, something that could restore me to the loving arms of the God of my younger years while accounting for everything that happened, that had changed me, since.

I found a book called *Grace Is Where I Live*.

I read it with thanks and caution, unwilling to give myself over fully, yet irresistibly drawn in. I saw in its pages glimpses of a path I might take; I felt the weight, though it would remain shapeless to me, of something like integrity. I emailed its author. I was certainly naïve and a little bothersome. You said, come walk with me.

When I conjure images of you, they are sometimes of us at Ace's Country Cupboard in Belfast or the like—those stalwart denizen diners of the Southern Tier—dipping the corners of buttery grilled cheese sandwiches into bowls of steaming minestrone against the cold afternoons. Oh how I loved those lunches every bit as much as high-end cuisine at any urban bistro.

I remember us sitting at a picnic table in Letchworth State Park, near the Mount Morris Dam. We'd hiked a decent hike, our steps accentuated by lines from Robert Bly or William Carlos Williams, and had come into a clearing. We sat down at the table. You took an apple from your pocket, shined it on your shirt, and began slicing it with a jackknife. You offered me slices while you ate others from the tip of the knife. This is you—earthy, unassuming, sagacious, and finally reverential, taking nothing for granted—this is what endures in my mind's eye. Oh, and you're funny. We laughed a lot! I think you knew it would be good for my deadly self-serious temperament.

I may be romanticizing, or simply shaping a story as I'm prone to do, but this is the truth as best I remember it, buoyed by gratitude, and I find it worthy of revisiting and sharing with younger readers who may feel a need and desire for a mentor.

There's a lot of food in this story, and that seems right. Each week after taking communion I say with my neighbors:

Alleluia. Christ our Passover is sacrificed for us;
Therefore let us keep the feast. Alleluia.

In the name of practicing what I preach—as I convey to my creative writing students the primacy of sensory images—let me end on one.

It's 2008. I am writing instructional design for a small e-learning company in the suburbs of Rochester, New York. It pays the bills, which is lovely, because we have a little one now and diapers aren't cheap. But I'm stalled out, depressed, anxious to get on with my writing life, what I think of as my *real* life, unable to see the goodness around me, to see the bigger picture. I'm a little like the young Van Gogh in his letter. I'm scared that it's already too late to make good on my professional and artistic dreams. I want, essentially, what I have now, but I don't dare even dream it.

Mike, you meet me for lunch as often as you can get away, and that sustains me through many tired winter afternoons. And Jack, you had secured a college vehicle to drive to Grand Rapids for the Festival of Faith and Writing. I have no right to be in this vehicle, but you offer me a ride anyway.

Shortly after arriving in Michigan, I find myself in rooms with serious literary practitioners talking in serious ways about making art and following Christ. Some are famous, others obscure (at least to me). Something shifts inside me over those few days.

I see my dream, my future, the one both of you had prepared me for. I find my tribe, my true home. I see something greater than I'd imagined.

On the final day, under a warm spring sun, I stagger exhausted onto a bench outside the Prince Center. I sit down. I begin to weep. I don't really know what all comprises these tears: joy, sadness, longing, a powerful vision. I must be a sight to any passersby because as I recall, the weeping is also half barbaric yawp. I positively lose it, give myself over to some primal instinct that cannot be expressed in language. I nearly rend some clothing.

Looking back, it's clear to me that the bench on the campus of Calvin College was a sacred space of initiation, a baptism into new life. Before one can be born again, one must die. In John's Gospel (12:24), Jesus says, "Unless a grain of wheat falls to the ground and dies, it remains just a grain of wheat; but if it dies, it produces much fruit." I'd suffered the death of the ego, the false self, which had me winning major book awards and being named to endowed chairs at colleges all by the ripe old age of, oh, let's say twenty-eight just to be safe. It turned out that my path to a place where my deep gladness could meet the world's deep hunger (Buechner again) would be more circuitous than I'd imagined. Isn't it always? You tried to tell me this, both of you, without hurting me, but the young are no good for such talk.

Just as I chipped in my widow's mite at those lovely feasts we kept together, this letter too is nothing more than a trifle. Maybe that's all I'll ever have to offer back.

Or perhaps my true offering is this: I'm the one footing the bill now (time, presence, sometimes money, love), for there are, by some wonder, those who come to me these days.

They need the same affirmations, the same conversations . . . or I should say that the substance of those talks is sometimes quite different. They have unique problems and concerns, as each generation must. But the spirit of our time together seems to me to be much the same. While I may not have live jazz or Mediterranean food here in my cornfield-flanked town—or even a ripe apple, a jackknife, and a sure hand—I've got what I've got to give: myself, a self you nurtured to be in this world.

There is more to say, and I promise to write to you both soon. In those notes we can talk about our families, our daily issues, and the rest of the wonderful, worthy stuff of life.

For now, as I began by saying thank you, I will end with the same to you both, and to our God. A prayer in the words of St. Thomas Aquinas:

All praise and thanks to Thee ascend
    For evermore, blest One in Three;
O grant us life that shall not end,
    In our true native land with Thee. Amen.

I'm grateful I can tell some of our stories here, especially for those who may need help seeing a way forward in their own lives, a path to their true native land.

Yours,
Dan

SEND AND THE FUTURE OF NEURODIVERSITY

In the spirit of hope I had a new idea.

I knew that when I spoke about autism, people listened. I wasn't the same person who did the Identity Intersections talk a few years before. I'd written more, spoken at events, and grown; I'd expanded on my early insights into autism and in my comfort level discussing it as an advocate.

I wondered if I could use my position to help others locally. Specifically: I felt it was time to connect with autistic students on my campus.

Perhaps now I was ready to give them glimpses of the labyrinth, as my mentors had done for me. I could affirm them and help normalize conversations about autism and autistic brains. I could pray with them and support them no matter what paths they chose. Maybe I could even bring healing.

I thought back to making culture in my small town through the arts center, adding to the "stock of available reality" in my community, providing a healthy outlet for learning, for the expression of feelings, and for the building of relationships.

I wanted to do it again: to make something.

I took to the internet, using the hashtag #TaylorU for visibility. I sent out some posts and tweets to the effect that I was starting a new campus group, a club for students on the spectrum. Within hours, I got a DM from a junior social studies ed major, Rachel, with whom I've since become good friends. She saw my tweet and reached out to say that she and a few others had formed a club already. They were going by the name SMHA: Students for Mental Health Awareness. She said that several club members were autistic.

Would I be interested in coming to a meeting? They were still getting their legs under them—in the middle of the process to be approved as an officially recognized university club—but they had already had some meetings and had staged events advocating for deeper understanding of neurodiversity and helpful mental health strategies for college students.

I jumped at the chance to join and soon was attending meetings. I was even asked to speak. A photographer and journalist from the campus newspaper came, and they did a story about us—a story that we were shaping through the power of our own voices.

Through discussions with the dean of students and others in residence life, the group ultimately came to a decision to narrow its focus from overall mental health to just neurodiversity. By the time the student senate was preparing to approve official club status, the students had decided to change the name to SEND: Students for Education on Neurodiversity. And they had articulated a mission statement: "SEND is dedicated to eradicating the stigma that surrounds neurodiversity of all sorts, through education and awareness, and encouraging a healthy mental lifestyle."

In their club constitution, they write:

We are passionate about neurodiversity. Everyone's brain is built differently, and we should celebrate those differences.

SEND will come together to help create a community and an atmosphere on campus where people can be free to be themselves without worrying about others' perceptions of them for things they cannot control. This will help to create a more unified community as people do not have to fear stigma and prejudice.

We will work toward this goal by raising awareness, educating, and advocating for acceptance. These activities may take the form of poster campaigns, events, and discussions.

In the coming months, I got to know the students in the group better by attending multiple meetings and helping plan events. The hallmark of the spring for me was a panel discussion on the intersection of the Enneagram and neurodiversity. SEND conceived of this idea as a way of coming to greater self-awareness. The Enneagram had been growing in popularity on our campus in recent years, and the autistic students thought: why don't we see how it can come into conversation with a neurodiversity paradigm to press us more deeply into understanding—and becoming better equipped to love—ourselves and our neighbors?

It was a huge idea, and the discussion included two certified Enneagram teachers, one of whom has a spouse on the spectrum and is extremely well versed in the tenets of neurodiversity. The level of the discourse rose above most undergraduate events I'd attended; the students had put together something on the cutting edge, the very frontiers of thinking about neurodiversity.

* * *

I loved getting to know the students in SEND through these events. But I wanted to hear more about their backgrounds; I wanted to talk especially with the autistics in the group to hear what it's like to go to college in the year 2020 as a diagnosed autistic. I wanted to know what it's like to go to our university in particular, one that prides itself on fostering intentional community. Did they feel they had a place in the campus community? Did they get overwhelmed by the social expectations or executive dysfunction? Also: how did they view God? Had their image of God changed or been shaped by their understanding of their differently wired brains?

I wanted to know all this and more. I wanted to know them so I could support and serve them both in and outside the classroom. I wanted to learn how their generation viewed autism. But also: I just really liked these young people.

So I asked them if anyone would want to be interviewed. Several were enthusiastic about sharing their experiences. I told them that some of it might be used in this book, but aside from that, it would be a blessing just to listen to them tell their stories.

. . .

Grace is a math major from Indianapolis. She's friendly and animated and pretty straightforward in demeanor, and she stims with a fidget cube as we chat. I ask about diagnosis. Her sister was an elementary ed major taking a class in special education, studying autism in particular. Her mom, a teacher at Grace's school, was also working with a student on the spectrum. A conversation began between Grace's mom and sister. The focus turned to Grace.

> They both came to the same conclusion: from what they were learning, they believed I was on the spectrum. They did more research and shared it with me. And I spent time reading all these articles and was like, "Ah. That makes sense." Then it became a special interest, looking up anything and everything associated with autism. It was very affirming to know why I experienced certain things differently. I think it took me a while to fully accept it, though. I didn't really talk to a lot of people about it at first.

Others' journeys were quite different, unfolding over the course of years. Matt is a sophomore psychology major. A handsome, thoughtful guy with close-cropped dark hair and glasses, he's passionate and engaged in the process of telling his story from the beginning. He says,

> It all started on Minecraft. I was thirteen. I was in this group chat and I think I said something socially unacceptable, and it made everyone leave the chat. And I was like, what the heck? One person decided to stay, she was sixteen. She asked me why I said what I said, and I just poured my heart out to her. I was always called annoying, creepy, weird, gay, retarded, whatever. And I wanted to know why. She brought up the idea that maybe I had a disorder.
>
> I vehemently denied it. I had always had it drilled into my head that nothing was wrong with me, that there could be nothing different about me.
>
> Fast forward to my junior year of high school when we started studying autism, and I was like, "Okay, that checks out, that checks out," as we looked at the traits. The one that really stood out was hyper-fixation. I was obsessed with ancient Egypt for four years! People always told me to stop talking about Egypt!

. . .

Rachel is the social studies ed major who clued me into the group to begin with; she's hyperverbal, smart, intense, and funny. She keeps me on my toes with roller-coaster descriptions, tangents, granular details, big-picture insights, and more. Her speech is punctuated by rhotacism, an inability to pronounce *r* sounds. She is simultaneously overwhelming and charming; I've liked her from the start.

In her case, a high school friend mentioned to her directly that she might have Asperger's. "I didn't know that was a thing. At first I got it confused with Alzheimer's!" she says, and we laugh.

She tells me more about the friend: how many theatrical productions they were in together, even some of the characters they played.

"So anyway," she picks up, "I'm trying to figure out what this thing is, I'm googling autism, and, not surprisingly . . . most of it made sense. Almost everything was . . . scarily accurate."

She goes on to say that when she told her mom, her mom said, "We thought you might be autistic, but we didn't tell you because we didn't want you to get placed into special ed."

"I was very high achieving, so I can see why she didn't want me to get lumped into a program I didn't need. Whether I agree with their decision not to tell me . . . that's something I'm still working through."

. . .

Beyond their diagnosis stories, we talked about stimming, about handling the stresses and anxieties of full-time university studies, about the gifts of neurodiversity as the students perceived them. Mostly they told me about their daily lives.

The students are so smart and generally upbeat. But their stories, like mine, are tinged with pain.

Tessa, a cybersecurity major from Kentucky, is perhaps the most openly autistic student I know; she tells many of her professors and peers upon meeting them. She also takes pleasure in educating people about the spectrum. I ask her, "What are some of the common misperceptions you've heard from people?" She says with a smile, "Sometimes I don't give people a chance to voice their misconceptions." We laugh. But then she tells me a story of a stranger who overheard a conversation in which she had disclosed her autism. The stranger berated her, saying that this person's brother was a "real" autistic and that Tessa's experience—her life—was not valid.

My own diagnosis has come into question a number of times in recent years, sometimes in an arrogant way and other times through more innocent inquiries. People tend to think that we're claiming some special status to try to be unique, and some are resentful and angry.

Autistic writer Sarah Kurchak addresses this situation in her whip-smart and hilarious book *I Overcame My Autism and All I Got Was This Lousy Anxiety Disorder*: "What people are really doing when they're trying to determine if I'm really autistic is figuring out if I make them uncomfortable or sad enough to count."[1]

Not long ago I read an article about David Byrne coming to terms with his autism. He's an iconic artist, opulently articulate, and self-aware. It was so empowering to learn that he's one of us. For some reason I scrolled down to the comments. I think I assumed I'd see some versions of, "Wow! How cool that he's autistic. I didn't know artists could be on the spectrum."

Instead, the first comment, the only one I read, said, "What a joke. He is so obviously not autistic." People have said the same of Hannah Gadsby and many other autistics in the public eye.

· · ·

One of the last questions I asked the students was, "How does your autism relate to your faith journey?" Most of these young people have been in churches their whole lives, so their answers were complex and diverse. We noted first that an incarnational, embodied understanding of Christ means that everything we'd been talking about up to that point was also God talk—that reflecting on our daily lives was indeed talking about our faith.

Grace mentioned how her roommate is very charismatic and dances during worship, while she feels more comfortable sitting quietly, away from others if possible. "Sometimes people will be, like, crying or on their knees, and I never know how to interact with them in those moments." I tell her I definitely connect with that feeling. She goes on to say that she loves science and that her faith has sometimes taken a more intellectual, rather than emotional, dimension. "It's the story that makes the most sense to me," she said of the arc of Christianity.

Tessa describes once visiting a friend's church, a Reformed church that believed in double predestination. She says that the Sunday school teacher shared a story about a case in point: his own son. He said that his son was autistic and nonverbal and had cerebral palsy, and since he could neither comprehend nor make a declaration of faith, he was predestined for hell. Sad, sure, but this Sunday school teacher had accepted it.

Well, Tessa could not.

I was only in middle school, but I was furious and I asked him all these questions. It was awful and it made me really mad. I knew it wasn't true. It was outlandish. So I wrestled with it.

Years later in a church service across the country I saw a man and his son. The son had cerebral palsy and I noticed he also had on ear defenders, so I thought he might be autistic. And his father was holding him gently . . . and I saw that I was watching someone translate the word of God into the heart-language of his son, and I knew that the gospel was not inaccessible. It's for all of us.

Sometimes churches make choices that don't include people with disabilities. We are going to do things differently, and that's okay. At a school I used to attend, we had mandatory chapel. At Taylor, it's not mandatory, so for those of us who need to listen to the audio and can't always be in the room, they're making it accessible for us. It's a small thing, but . . . churches need to listen to the people in their congregations and find ways to accommodate them, to make the gospel accessible.

. . .

Matt recalls the bullying he experienced when he was younger and the heavy burden of carrying that emotional baggage, "the baggage of unforgiveness, the baggage of self-hatred." He says, "Finally you have to decide to see yourself through God's eyes. God can work through our autism. He can use it to meet the basic human need for connection—the rate of suicide with autistics, I think bonding and community can help with that."

As we finish the interview, he says, "I think it's really hard to love yourself when society has told you that you're unlovable. So . . . I did this thing where I had some index cards, and I wrote down nice things that people have said about me. . . . I committed those cards to memory, because I've heard it said that all truth is God's truth. If you can learn to love yourself, I think it gives rise to the confidence to love others. I think it's especially important for neurodivergent people, because it can be so hard to accept and love ourselves."

When Rachel begins to speak about her faith, she mentions two foundations: loving your neighbor as yourself, and the good Samaritan. The future educator says,

> As I take on more leadership roles on campus, it's the idea of trying to become the person you needed. That's what I am trying to do: be for others the person I needed when I was in their place. Trying to notice others who need someone, and reach out to them. Trying to make a place where people can go. And trying to establish something that will last longer than me.
>
> There are people saying they love me but also that they want to cure autism. Where do I end and the autism begins? Without autism, would I be me? How can we call it Christian community if we don't accept some of the people as . . . legitimate? Living in Christian community . . . we can't do that unless we're living with *everyone*.

. . .

Each of these students helps me to see myself through God's eyes and to be a better member of our community. Spending time with them, I learn to love my neighbor because I keep learning to love myself. The students of SEND minister to me as much as I could ever minister to them. They remind me over and over that grace is not merely transactional, but relational.

ACKNOWLEDGMENTS

I will always thank Bethany, Una, and Casey first. I can't believe I get to have you for my family. I'm eternally grateful.

Thank you, Mom and Dad, for your love and support, and thank you, Gail and Paul, my other mom and dad, for your love and support; thank you to each of my Bowman and Whittaker siblings.

Thank you to my students at Taylor University; it's an honor to work alongside you. Thank you to my colleagues, especially Dr. Nancy Dayton, chair of the English department, for making space for me to be me.

Thank you to my dear friend and coconspirator Dr. Aaron Housholder. You know me better than anyone on campus. I couldn't do any of the things I get to do without you, and I wouldn't want to.

Thank you to my agent, Keely Boeving, for taking a chance on me, for believing in my work, and for encouragement and insight; you make me better. Thank you to Katelyn Beaty for seeing the potential in this book and strengthening it many times over. Thank you to the wonderful team at Brazos for your kindness and expertise at every turn.

Thank you, Tania and Marci and Brad and every one of you deliciously incorrigible Woodland Creatures. How I love you. Thank you, Amy and Jack, Justin and Tracy, Adele and Josh, John and Abi, Josh and Michelle, Jeff and Jane, Scott and Jennifer, Josh and Aimee, Nick and Beth. Thank you, Kia. Thank you, Reverend Julia. Thank you, Mother Mindy and all at Gethsemane Church.

Thank you to you whom I've been privileged to call friend.

Thank you to the editors of the following journals where earlier versions of these essays first appeared: *Art House America* ("A True Name," "Dancing in Fields of Wheat and Tares," "Meaning and Estrangement," "Peace in Terabithia," "Shining like the Sun"); *Books & Culture* ("Living Maps"); *Christianity Today: This Is Our City* ("Autistic Culture Making"); *Facts & Trends* ("Autism and Church"); *Fieldnotes: Practical Wisdom for Emerging Leaders* ("Therefore Let Us Keep the Feast"); *Good Letters: The Image Journal Blog* ("Beautiful Loser"); *The Mighty* ("Diversity and Dignity"); *Relief* ("The Tracks of My Tears," "Loving the Expanse"); *Ruminate* ("Alienation and Symbol," "The Insidious Nature of Bad Christian Stories," "Riding while Autistic," "Speaking the Words," "Spectrum Interview: Brian"); and *TweetSpeak* ("Autism and Poetry").

NOTES

Prelude

1. "Autistic Adults Thought They Were 'Bad People,'" *Neuroscience News*, November 7, 2019, https://neurosciencenews.com/asd-adults-bad-15180, citing Steven Stagg and Hannah Belcher, "Living with Autism without Knowing: Receiving a Diagnosis in Later Life," *Health Psychology and Behavioral Medicine* 7, no. 1 (2019): 348–61, https://doi.org/10.1080/21642850.2019.1684920.

2. Ann Griswold, "Large Swedish Study Ties Autism to Early Death," *Spectrum*, December 11, 2015, https://www.spectrum news.org/news/large-swedish-study-ties-autism-to-early-death; and Michael A. Ellis, "Early Death in Those with Autism Spectrum Disorder," *Psychology Today*, October 7, 2018, https://www.psychologytoday.com/us/blog/caring-autism/201810/early-death-in-those-autism-spectrum-disorder.

3. Ashlea McKay, "The M Word: We Need to Talk about Adult Autistic Meltdowns," *Medium*, September 25, 2017, https://medium.com/@AshleaMcKay/the-m-word-we-need-to-talk-about-adult-autistic-meltdowns-fec98f60157b.

4. Kaleb Johnson, "What Meltdowns Feel Like as an Adult on the Autism Spectrum," *Yahoo! Finance*, April 24, 2018, https://

finance.yahoo.com/news/meltdowns-feel-adult-autism-spectrum
-230412791.html.

5. Paula D'Arcy, quoted in Richard Rohr, *Everything Belongs: The Gift of Contemplative Prayer* (New York: Crossroad, 2003), 130.

6. David Finch, *The Journal of Best Practices: A Memoir of Marriage, Asperger Syndrome, and One Man's Quest to Be a Better Husband* (New York: Simon & Schuster, 2012), 4–6.

7. Julie Brown, *Writers on the Spectrum: How Autism and Asperger Syndrome Have Influenced Literary Writing* (London: Jessica Kingsley, 2010), 7.

8. Cynthia Kim, *Nerdy, Shy, and Socially Inappropriate: A User Guide to an Asperger Life* (London: Jessica Kingsley, 2015), 19.

9. Brown, *Writers on the Spectrum*, 31.

Why You Should Read This Book (and How)

1. "CDC Estimates 2.2 Percent of Adults in U.S. Have Autism," Autism Speaks, May 13, 2020, https://www.autismspeaks.org/science-news/cdc-estimates-22-percent-adults-us-have-autism.

2. For a more comprehensive understanding of this, read Steve Silberman, *NeuroTribes: The Legacy of Autism and the Future of Neurodiversity* (New York: Penguin Random House, 2015).

3. Julie Brown, *Writers on the Spectrum: How Autism and Asperger Syndrome Have Influenced Literary Writing* (London: Jessica Kingsley, 2010), 21, 23, quoting Stuart Murray, *Representing Autism: Culture, Narrative, Fascination* (Liverpool: Liverpool University Press, 2008), 5.

4. Thea Temple, "Why a Literate Culture Is Important, or Why I Founded the Writer's Garret," *Langdon Review of the Arts in Texas* 2 (2005): 49, 63.

5. Nell Brown, "This Love," in *Stim: An Autistic Anthology*, ed. Lizzie Huxley-Jones (London: Unbound, 2020), 63.

Diversity and Dignity

1. Wikipedia, s.v. "Temple Grandin," last modified December 4, 2020, https://en.wikipedia.org/wiki/Temple_Grandin.

2. Chimamanda Ngozi Adichie, "The Danger of a Single Story," TED, July 2009, https://www.ted.com/talks/chimamanda_ngozi _adichie_the_danger_of_a_single_story.

Speaking the Words

1. Quoted in Ioan James, "Singular Scientists," *Journal of the Royal Society of Medicine* 96, no. 1 (January 2003): 36–39.

A Portrait of the Autist as a Young Man

1. Elyse Wanshel, "YouTuber Gave Up Adopted Chinese Son with Autism after Monetizing Him Online," *Huffington Post*, May 28, 2020, https://www.huffpost.com/entry/myka-stauffer-adopted -chinese-son-autism_n_5ed00446c5b6521c93a80e07.

2. Zack Linly, "Florida Woman Arrested for Drowning Her Autistic Son after Telling Police Two Black Men Abducted Him," *The Root*, May 26, 2020, https://www.theroot.com/florida -woman-arrested-for-drowning-her-autistic-son-af-1843683283.

The Neurodiversity Paradigm

1. Janice Rodden, "What Does Autism Spectrum Disorder Look Like in Adults?," *ADDitude Magazine*, updated October 14, 2020, https://www.additudemag.com/autism-spectrum-disorder-in-adults.

2. Melissa Conrad Stöppler, "Autism: Symptoms and Signs," MedicineNet, https://www.medicinenet.com/autism_symptoms _and_signs/symptoms.htm.

3. Autistic Self Advocacy Network, "About Autism," https:// autisticadvocacy.org/about-asan/about-autism.

4. Erik Engdahl, "What Is NT?," December 25, 2010, http:// erikengdahl.se/autism/isnt.

5. Barry Prizant, *Uniquely Human: A Different Way of Seeing Autism* (New York: Simon & Schuster, 2015), 6.

6. Nick Walker, "Throw Away the Master's Tools: Liberating Ourselves from the Pathology Paradigm," in *Loud Hands: Autistic People, Speaking*, ed. Julia Bascom (Washington, DC: Autism Self Advocacy Network, 2012). A revised version of this chapter appears in "Throw Away the Master's Tools: Liberating

Ourselves from the Pathology Paradigm," *Neurocosmopolitanism*, August 16, 2013, https://neurocosmopolitanism.com/throw-away-the-masters-tools-liberating-ourselves-from-the-pathology-paradigm.

Living Maps

1. Sarah Kurchak, "Some Autistic People Find Comfort in Specific Objects. What Happens When They're Not Available Anymore?," *Vox*, October 4, 2019, https://www.vox.com/the-goods/2019/10/4/20891450/autism-comfort-items-replacement-strategies.

2. Mary Oliver, "Ghosts," in *American Primitive* (New York: Little, Brown, 1983), 28.

3. Scott Russell Sanders, *Writing from the Center* (Bloomington: Indiana University Press, 1995), 8.

4. Quoted in Sanders, *Writing from the Center*, 5.

5. Alfred Kazin, *On Native Grounds: An Interpretation of Modern American Prose Literature* (New York: Mariner Books, 1995), 37–38.

6. Sanders, "Imagining the Midwest," in *Writing from the Center*, 38.

7. Barry Lopez, "A Literature of Place," *Portland Magazine* (Summer 1997), available at https://uwosh.edu/sirt/wp-content/uploads/sites/86/2020/04/Lopez_ALiteratureOfPlace.pdf.

8. Chinua Achebe, *Things Fall Apart* (London: William Heinemann, 1962), 3.

9. Norbert Krapf, *Bloodroot: Indiana Poems* (Bloomington, IN: Quarry Books, 2008), xvii.

10. Krapf, *Bloodroot*, 165.

11. Krapf, *Bloodroot*, 101. Poem used by permission of Indiana University Press.

12. "Reports on the Course of Instruction in Yale College; by a Committee of the Corporation, and the Academical Faculty," New Haven, CT, printed by Hezekiah Howe, 1828, available at https://collegiateway.org/reading/yale-report-1828. This report is commonly known as "The Yale Report of 1828."

Autistic Culture Making

1. Gregory Wolfe, "The Stock of Available Reality," *Image*, issue 26, https://imagejournal.org/article/the-stock-of-available-reality.

Riding while Autistic

1. "Stimming: What Autistic People Do to Feel Calmer," BBC News—Blogs, June 5, 2013, https://www.bbc.com/news/blogs-ouch-22771894.

Shining like the Sun

1. Thomas Merton, *Conjectures of a Guilty Bystander* (New York: Doubleday, 1996), 155.

2. Makoto Fujimura, *Refractions: A Journey of Faith, Art, and Culture* (Colorado Springs: NavPress, 2009).

3. Alan W. Jones, *Reimagining Christianity: Reconnect Your Spirit without Disconnecting Your Mind* (Hoboken, NJ: Wiley & Sons, 2004), 12.

4. "Works with Soul: Dave Harrity," *Ruminate: The Waking* (blog), April 5, 2012, https://www.ruminatemagazine.com/blogs/ruminate-blog/works-with-soul-dave-harrity.

Service and the Spectrum

1. "Marion, Indiana (IN) Poverty Rate Data," accessed December 11, 2020, http://www.city-data.com/poverty/poverty-Marion-Indiana.html.

2. Jessica Semega, Melissa Kollar, Emily A. Shrider, and John Creamer, "Income and Poverty in the United States: 2019," United States Census Bureau, September 15, 2020, https://www.census.gov/library/publications/2020/demo/p60-270.html.

Dancing in Fields of Wheat and Tares

1. Richard Rohr, *Things Hidden: Scripture as Spirituality* (London: SPCK, 2016), 25.

2. Quoted in Bessie Akuba Winn-Afeku, "The Role of an Artist Is to Not Look Away," *HuffPost*, updated December 6, 2017, https://www.huffpost.com/entry/the-role-of-an-artist-is-_b_4056141.

Autism and Poetry

1. John Gardner, *The Art of Fiction: Notes on Craft for Young Writers* (New York: Vintage, 1991), 87.

The Insidious Nature of Bad Christian Stories

1. Ron Hansen, *A Stay against Confusion: Essays on Faith and Fiction* (New York: Harper Perennial, 2002), 25.

2. John Gardner, *On Moral Fiction* (New York: Basic Books, 1979).

3. Anne Lamott, *Plan B: Further Thoughts on Faith* (New York: Riverhead, 2006), 256–57.

4. The phrase "negative capability" is used by John Keats in a letter to his brothers, George and Thomas Keats, December 22, 1817, available at https://en.wikisource.org/wiki/Letter_to _George_and_Thomas_Keats,_December_28,_1817.

5. "About Taylor University," accessed December 11, 2020, https://www.taylor.edu/about.

6. Richard Rohr, "Owning Our Cultural Biases," *Franciscan Spirit* (blog), May 7, 2020, https://www.franciscanmedia.org /franciscan-spirit-blog/owning-our-cultural-biases.

7. Enuma Okoro, "Faith Imitates Art," *Boundless*, April 19, 2007, https://www.boundless.org/faith/faith-imitates-art.

Beautiful Loser

1. Thomas Hardy, "During Wind and Rain," Poetry Foundation, https://www.poetryfoundation.org/poems/52314/during -wind-and-rain.

2. Mark Doty, "Tide of Voices: Why Poetry Matters Now," August 8, 2010, https://poets.org/text/tide-voices-why-poetry-matters-now.

3. Richard Rohr, *Falling Upward: A Spirituality for the Two Halves of Life* (San Francisco: Jossey-Bass, 2011).

Meaning and Estrangement

1. John Gardner, *On Becoming a Novelist* (New York: Norton, 1999), 77.

2. Alec Michod, "An Interview with Richard Powers," *The Believer*, February 1, 2007, https://believermag.com/an-interview -with-richard-powers.

3. Anne Lamott, *Plan B: Further Thoughts on Faith* (New York: Riverhead, 2006), 256–57.

A True Name

1. Most information on the Palatine migration, including my family genealogy, in this essay comes from Henry Jones Jr.'s comprehensive *The Palatine Families of New York 1710*, 2 vols. (Universal City, CA: H. Z. Jones, 1985).

2. Diane Mapes, "Bed-Wetting Blues: Millions of Adults Suffer, Too," NBC News, February 18, 2009, https://www.nbcnews.com /health/health-news/bed-wetting-blues-millions-adults-suffer-too -flna1C9452161.

3. Mapes, "Bed-Wetting Blues."

4. Brené Brown, "Shame v. Guilt," Brené Brown.com, January 14, 2013, https://brenebrown.com/blog/2013/01/14/shame-v-guilt.

5. Morgane Michael, "Shame vs. Humiliation vs. Guilt vs. Embarrassment (Brené Brown)," *Small Act Big Impact*, June 15, 2019, https://smallactbigimpact.com/2019/06/15/shame-vs-humiliation -vs-guilt-vs-embarrassment-brene-brown.

6. "Last Name: Baumann," accessed December 12, 2020, https://www.surnamedb.com/Surname/Baumann.

7. Henry Jones Jr., *Palatine Families of New York 1710*, 2:ix–x.

8. J. B. Cheaney, "The Power of Naming," *World Magazine*, November 7, 2011, https://world.wng.org/2011/11/the_power_of _naming.

9. Cheaney, "The Power of Naming."

10. Walker Percy, "Naming and Being," *Personalist* 41, no. 2 (April 1960), https://onlinelibrary.wiley.com/doi/epdf/10.1111 /j.1468-0114.1960.tb03646.x.

11. Lisa Nichols Hickman, "The Power of Naming," *Faith & Leadership*, September 12, 2011, https://faithandleadership.com /lisa-nichols-hickman-power-naming.

Peace in Terabithia

1. Chris Ware, "Jimmy Corrigan the Smartest Kid on Earth," *New Yorker*, June 12, 2000, https://www.newyorker.com/magazine/2000/06/19/jimmy-corrigan-the-smartest-kid-on-earth.

2. Arnold Weinstein, "Don't Turn Away from the Art of Life," *New York Times*, February 23, 2016, https://www.nytimes.com/2016/02/24/opinion/dont-turn-away-from-the-art-of-life.html.

Interview by Jenna

1. "About," Learn from Autistics, accessed December 12, 2020, https://www.learnfromautistics.com/about.

Interview by Brian

1. Thomas Armstrong, "Neurodiversity: A Concept Whose Time Has Come," *American Institute for Learning and Human Development*, accessed December 12, 2020, https://www.institute4learning.com/resources/articles/neurodiversity.

2. Armstrong, "Neurodiversity."

Falling and Autistic Representation

1. Katherine May, "Autism from the Inside," *Aeon Magazine*, August 22, 2018, https://aeon.co/essays/the-autistic-view-of-the-world-is-not-the-neurotypical-cliche.

2. Stephen Unwin, "All in a Row," *Stephen Unwin*, March 1, 2019, http://www.stephenunwin.uk/thoughts-and-provocations/2019/3/1/all-in-a-row.

3. May, "Autism from the Inside."

4. "Mr. Rogers Post Goes Viral," PBS News Hour, December 18, 2012, https://www.pbs.org/newshour/nation/fred-rogers-post-goes-viral.

Therefore Let Us Keep the Feast

1. Joseph Campbell, *The Hero with a Thousand Faces*, 3rd ed. (Novato, CA: New World Library, 2008), 18.

2. Makoto Fujimura, *Refractions: A Journey of Faith, Art, and Culture* (Colorado Springs: NavPress, 2009), 10.

SEND and the Future of Neurodiversity

1. Sarah Kurchak, *I Overcame My Autism and All I Got Was This Lousy Anxiety Disorder* (Medeira Park, BC: Douglas and McIntyre, 2020), 5.